To my lovely grandsons Cailean and Lewis

Pride of the Three Lions

Football's Comin' Home!

Derek Niven

By the Same Author

Pride of the Lions
Pride of the Jocks
Pride of the Bears
Pride of the Hearts

Writing as Derek Beaugarde

2084: The End of Days
2112: Revelation
2048 BCE: The Eye of Horus

Pride of the Three Lions

The untold story of the men and women
who made the heroes of Wembley 1966

Derek Niven

Corkerhill Press

Published in 2023 by Corkerhill Press

Copyright © Derek Niven 2023

ISBN Paperback - 978-1-7393929-0-1
EBook - 978-1-7393929-1-8

Front cover illustrations by Wheech © 2023

Ticket stub and Final programme
by permission of George McDonald

Lord Street photo by permission of Gainsborough Heritage Centre

Published with the help of Indie Authors World

IndieAuthors
World

ACKNOWLEDGEMENTS

The author wishes to acknowledge the valued assistance of Indie Authors World partners Sinclair and Kim Macleod and assisted by Rachel Hessin in the publishing of this book. Thanks to my editor Gillian Murphy for her usual studious efforts. A special thanks to friends John Steele and Robin Dale, who initially encouraged me to 'kick on' with this idea.

Particular thanks go to my ASGRA colleague Ian Marson, a professional genealogist based in Yorkshire, and a member of AGRA, for sharing his corroborative research on Gordon Banks ancestry. 'Todah' to the Sandy's Row Synagogue for help with George Cohen's Jewish ancestry.

Thanks also to the late Sir Dirk Bogarde for the pseudonym and our old alumni Allan Glen's School for the superb education.

Finally, without the unswerving love, support and patience of my wife Linda this book would never have seen the light of day.

Psalms 104:21 – The young lions roar after their prey, and seek their meat from God.

Contents

Contents

PREFACE

The casual Pride Series reader may think this latest book is about the great game of football. On the contrary, this publication is again about fate and destiny.

It examines the chance accumulation of fateful unions between men and women from the early 19th century. This culminated in the procreation of a remarkable group of young men, who wrote themselves into the history books nearly 60 years ago in the summer of 1966. It is about men and women who were born around 50 years before the formation of the newly formed England international association football club in 1870. They played their first official game against Scotland on 30 November 1872. These were ancestors who were brought together by destiny, unaware their descendants would be immortalised over a hundred years after their own births in the mid-19th century.

It could be argued this book not only celebrates the 57th anniversary of the Three Lions of 1966. It also marks the 153rd anniversary of the England team's foundation in 1870. There have been many high points in English international football history, however, 1966's World Cup victory at Wembley is always seen as the greatest achievement.

On a hot, sunny afternoon on 30 July 1966 at Wembley Stadium, London, eleven young Englishmen created footballing history by beating their ultimate arch-rivals, the mighty West Germany, 4–2 to lift the World Cup, the Jules Rimet trophy, and the most prestigious honour in the footballing world. They were the first and only English side to achieve such a feat. The legend of the Three Lions was born.

Looking at the exorbitantly paid international players developed nowadays around the globe who compete for the World Cup, it can be quickly realised. Never again will a team of local working-class lads win such a coveted trophy. Billions are now spent trying to wrest the most sought after award on the planet. This makes the Three Lions feat even more remarkable and unique.

Much has been written about that famous campaign in 1966 culminating in the final game at Wembley, played in front of a young Queen Elizabeth II. Minute detail documents the momentous game starting with Helmut Haller's 12th minute goal which Jack Charlton and Gordon Banks failed to stop. In the 18th minute a free kick crossed in by Bobby Moore was headed in for 1–1 by Geoff Hurst.

In the 77th minute a corner by Alan Ball found Hurst, and his deflected shot was turned in by Martin Peters. However, with only a minute left of normal time a scrambled effort in the England defence allowed Wolfgang Weber to equalise at 2–2 and force extra-time. In the 11th minute of extra-time a rasping shot by Geoff Hurst rattled off the bar, bouncing down behind the beaten German goalkeeper. The goal was awarded by the Russian linesman and is remembered as the most disputed goal in World Cup history. England 3–2.

With only a minute left to play and the Germans throwing everyone forward, Bobby Moore picked out an unmarked Hurst. Many spectators, thinking the whistle had blown, streamed onto the pitch-side. Undeterred, Hurst pressed on and blasted the winner home for a 4–2 victory. This gave rise to one of the most famous quotes in English footballing history, from BBC commentator Kenneth Wolstenholme: *"And here comes Hurst. He's got...some people are on the pitch... they think it's all over. It is now!"*

All that detail, eagerly sought by England aficionados, has been written, much more succinctly than myself, by footballing authors and sports journalists. The author is a professional genealogist and member of ASGRA. The reader may ask what brought a Scottish genealogist to want to write the Three Lions family histories.

As a young boy of ten, the author and his family sat glued to the tiny Phillips black and white television, with only two channels, BBC and ITV. They watched England beat mighty West Germany. He'll never forget how sunny and warm it was that Saturday, even in Glasgow. His father sent him out at half time to the local Wall's general store on Corkerhill Road to purchase cigarettes. Unbelievable now, Wall's happily sold a pack of Embassy Tipped to a ten year old, knowing it was for a parent. He ran like the wind to get back in time for the second half.

Even in Scotland, the streets were eerily empty and there was virtually no traffic as he ran to Wall's. It might surprise English fans to know that, after the game, many Scots joined in the celebrations. He fully remembers that beautiful summer evening playing football with his pals on the Corkerhill railway village green. They all wanted to be Bobby Moore or Geoff Hurst. However, it was in the following year the journey towards the Pride Series of football history books began to crystallise.

On 25 May 1967, his mother Rita took him, aged eleven, up to his Gran McCue's high-rise flat in Pollokshaws, in south-west Glasgow. Granny Annie Collie was Protestant, although his Grandpa Frank McCue and Uncle Jim, were Catholic. As his mother chatted away to her mother Annie, the 'men' sat enthralled, watching the historic game unfold on the small telly. Glasgow Celtic became the first British side to lift the European Cup, defeating mighty Inter Milan 2–1. At the age of eleven, he was too young to travel to football games on his own, so he did not immediately become a Celtic fan.

Fate lent a hand.

His father Archie was an ardent Rangers supporter and wanted him to follow the Teddy Bears. To that end, on 7 September 1969, his father took him to Ibrox Park to watch Rangers face Polish side Gornik Zabrze in a UEFA Cup Winners' Cup second leg match. Rangers trailed 3–1 from the first leg, although there was significant optimism manager Davie White's side would easily overcome that score in the return match at home. That optimism was totally dispelled that damp winter evening when Rangers were defeated by another 3–1 and lost 6–2 to Gornik. The defeat ended Davie White's managerial career. As his father trudged despondently back from Ibrox Park to Corkerhill, Archie uttered these fateful words, *'I'll never be back at Ibrox again.'* Although the author has a copy of the match programme, given to him on his retirement from the railway industry in 2007 by colleague, DJ Steeley, it seems to serve as a reminder of his father's dismissive words and Rangers was not the team for him at that point in his life.

Celtic continued to dominate Scottish football. They were on course for a record-breaking nine-in-a-row league titles and another final appearance in the European Cup against the Dutch team Feyenoord in 1970. Celtic was the team to support. His Protestant father did not object, although deep down he would rather see his son go to Ibrox. It was the support for Celtic dating back to 1967 that inspired him to write the first book in the Pride Series: Pride of the Lions, the untold story of the men and women who made the Lisbon Lions.

Pride of the Three Lions celebrates the 57th anniversary of the 1966 team. This is not from a footballing perspective, but from a genealogical, familial, religious and social history perspective. It relates the history of the Three Lions from the viewpoint of the people who created that unique group of players, i.e., their direct ancestors. This is from the perspective of their origins, lives, loves and occupations.

The author's family history is a tale of poor, struggling agricultural labourers, coal miners and railway workers striving to achieve more than their working class existence afforded them. Within his own history are tales of heroism through two world wars, tales of illegitimacy, infant mortality, the poorhouse and grinding poverty. The average reader will be able to see their family history in the same vein.

Likewise, the genealogy of the Three Lions of '66 reveals a remarkably similar story of ordinary working class boys from predominantly poor backgrounds who achieved something extraordinary. It has not been possible to research every aspect of the lives of the ancestors of the Three Lions. In the main the detailed research concentrates on their English family history, generally back to the early 1800s. The reader may be surprised to find there is also a smattering of Scottish, Irish, Welsh and Eastern European ancestry coursing through the veins of the Wembley heroes. Although most of the players have now passed on to that great stadium in the sky, the Three Lions remain immortal, even within the confines of this book.

The Three Lions of 1966.

This is their amazing story.

CHAPTER 1

Gordon Banks OBE (Goalkeeper)

Honours as an England player:
1 FIFA World Cup winner 1966
1 EUFA European Championship (Bronze medallist) 1968
8 British Home Championships

G ordon Banks OBE was born on 30 December 1937 at 15 Arthur Road, Abbeydale, Sheffield, Yorkshire, to parents Thomas Banks and Nellie Yates. Gordon was registered in 1st Quarter 1938 (Sheffield, 9C/893). He was an English professional footballer who played as a goalkeeper. He made 679 appearances during a 20-year professional career, and won 73 caps for England, highlighted by starting every game of the 1966 World Cup victory.

Banks was raised in the working class area of Tinsley at 138 Ferrars Road and attended Tinsley County Secondary

Modern School. In 1948, when Banks was 11, the family moved to Catcliffe village after his father Thomas opened a betting shop. As a youth Banks played for Sheffield Schoolboys, and left school in December 1952, aged 15, to take up employment as a coal merchant's bagger. This work helped build his upper body strength. Banks waited in the coal lorry as the coal trains entered Tinsley Yard. The baggers got into the wagons, shovelling coal into bags and stacking them on the lorry. They delivered the sacks to homes and businesses around Sheffield.

Banks spent a season playing for amateur side Millspaugh, after their regular goalkeeper failed to show. His performances earned him a place in the Yorkshire League for Rawmarsh Welfare, however a 12–2 defeat on his debut was followed by a 3–1 home defeat, and he was dropped by Rawmarsh and returned to Millspaugh. Still aged 15, his brother David spoke up for him and Gordon became a bricklayer's hod-carrier.

Chesterfield scouted him while playing for Millspaugh and offered a six-game trial in the youth team in March 1953. He impressed enough to be offered a part-time £3-a-week contract by manager Teddy Davison in July 1953. The reserve team were placed in the Central League. Banks conceded 122 goals in 1954–55 as the 'Spireites' finished in last place with only three victories. Aged 18, Banks was posted to Germany with the Royal Corps of Signals on national service, winning the Rhine Cup with his regimental team. He recovered from a fractured elbow to help the Chesterfield youth team to the 1956 FA Youth Cup final.

They were beaten 4–3 on aggregate by Manchester United's ill-fated 'Busby Babes', including Wilf McGuinness and Bobby Charlton.

Banks made his first team debut for Chesterfield in November 1958 and was sold to Leicester City for £7,000 in July 1959. He played in four cup finals for the club, losing in the 1961 and 1963 FA Cup finals. He won the League Cup in 1964, finishing as beaten finalists in 1965. Banks is best remembered as Alf Ramsey's first choice goalkeeper in the 1966 World Cup campaign. Banks played in every match during the finals, culminating in victory against West Germany.

Despite these successes, and his famous World Cup win, he was dropped by Leicester and sold to Stoke City for £50,000 in April 1967. In the 1970 World Cup finals in Mexico, he arguably made one of the game's greatest ever saves to prevent a certain Pelé goal. Banks was absent due to illness as England were beaten by West Germany at the quarter-final stage.

Banks was Stoke City's goalkeeper in the 1972 League Cup win, the club's only major honour. He was still Stoke and England's number one when a car crash in October 1972 cost him both his right eye sight, and eventually, his career. He played two final seasons in the United States for the Fort Lauderdale Strikers in 1977 and 1978. Despite only having vision in one eye, he was NASL Goalkeeper of the Year in 1977. He briefly managed Telford United before retiring from football in December 1980. Regarded as one of the greatest goalkeepers of all time, Banks was named FWA

Footballer of the Year in 1972. He was FIFA Goalkeeper of the Year on six occasions.

Gordon's parents –
Thomas Banks and Nellie H Yates

Gordon's father Thomas Banks aka Tommy was born on 28 May 1906 in Tinsley, a bustling railway and steelworks suburb of north-east Sheffield, Yorkshire to parents John Edward Banks and Emma Etta Johnson (Rotherham, 9C/734). In 1911, Tommy, 4, at school, at the Tinsley Hotel, Carbrook, Sheffield, with father John Edward Banks, 43, a hotel keeper, mother Etty, 42, assisting in the business, and his siblings.

Gordon's mother Nellie Yates was born on 27 August 1909 in Lincolnshire to parents William Edwin Yates and Kate Etherington (Gainsborough, 7A/688). In 1911, Nellie, 1, at 6 Hooton's Buildings, Gainsborough, with father William Edwin Yates, 51, a butcher, mother Kate, 44, and her siblings. By 1921, Nellie, 11, at school, was living in Sheffield, Yorkshire with father William Edwin Yates, mother Kate, and her siblings.

Thomas Banks married wife Nellie H Yates in 4th Quarter 1927 (Sheffield, 9C/1422). Thomas and Nellie had 4 known sons in Sheffield; John Richard (b. 26 March 1931, disabled), Michael (b. 3 Q. 1932), David (b. 4 May 1934) and Gordon (b. 30 December 1937). Son Gordon Banks was born on 30 December 1937 at 15 Arthur Road, Abbeydale (Sheffield, 9C/146).

Thomas and Nellie raised their family in the working-class area of Tinsley, known for its huge railway freight marshalling yard and large steelworks, both dominating the district. In 1939 War Register, Thomas Banks, born 26 May 1906, a steelwork slinger, at 138 Ferrars Road, Tinsley, Sheffield, with wife Nellie, born 27 August 1909, doing unpaid domestic duties, sons John Richard, born 26 March 1931, David, born 4 May 1934, both at school, and two other sons classed as 'record officially closed'. As Gordon was born in 1937, he is one of the closed records.

In 1948, the family moved to Catcliffe village after Thomas opened a betting shop. This brought prosperity to the family, but also tragedy. Three years after seeing his son Gordon lift the 1966 World Cup at Wembley, Thomas Banks, 63, died in 1969 in Rotherham. In 1971, Thomas' disabled son John, 40, was severely mugged for the betting shop's daily takings. John died of his injuries some weeks later on 1 August 1971. Nellie Banks nee Yates, 84, died in April 1984 in Rotherham.

Gordon's paternal grandparents –
John Edward Banks and Emma Etta Johnson

Gordon's paternal grandfather John Edward Banks was born in 1st Quarter 1873 in Atherton, Lancashire, to parents Thomas Scowcroft Banks, an innkeeper, and Margaret Hunter (Leigh, 8C/263). John and his sister, Ellen, were baptized together on 7 September 1873 in Hoole Church. Gordon's England teammate Roger Hunt's ancestry was also strongly associated with Leigh. John's father Thomas Scowcroft Banks died in 1886 and his widowed mother Margaret was left to run the family hostelry. In 1891, John E, 17, an assistant hotel employee, resided and worked at the Punch Bowl Hotel, Market Street, Atherton, with his widowed mother Margaret Banks, 53, a publican, and his siblings, most of whom also worked in the hotel.

Gordon's grandmother Emma Hetty Johnson, aka Etta or Etty, was born in 2nd Quarter 1876 in Brightside, Sheffield. John Edward Banks, a publican, married Emma Etta Johnson in 1st Quarter 1899 (Rotherham, 9C/737). John and Emma had 7 known children; in Tyldesley, Jack (b. 4 November 1899), Lawrence (b. 6 December 1900); in Tinsley, Sheffield, Harry (b. 3 Q. 1903, d. 1 January 1904), Joseph aka Joe (b. 3 June 1905), Tommy (b. 28 May 1906), Dorothy (b. 3 February 1908) and George (b. 30 November 1916). Son Thomas Banks was born on 28 May 1906 in Tinsley, Sheffield (Rotherham, 8C/734).

In 1901, John Edward Banks, 25, lived and worked as a publican in the Prince of Wales Inn, Elliot Street, Tyldesley, with wife Etty, 24, sons Jack, 1, and Lawrence, 4 months old, employing a domestic servant Mary Wainwright, 21. By 1903 the Banks family had moved to Tinsley, Sheffield.

In 1911, John Edward Banks, 43, ran the Tinsley Hotel, Carbrook, Sheffield, with wife Etty, 42, assisting in the business, children Jack, 11, Lawrence, 10, Joseph, 5, Tommy, 4, all at school, and Dorothy, 3. Also assisting in the hotel business were Aggie Clark, 19, a barmaid, Maggie Fletcher, 17, Dorothy Jenkinson, 17, and Mabel Purt, 16, all domestic servants. In 1921, John Edward Banks, 49, still lived in Tinsley, Attercliffe, Sheffield with wife Emma, 48, children Joe, 16, Tommy, 15, Dorothy, 13, and George, 4. The Tinsley Hotel stood on the main Rotherham to Sheffield Road opposite the steelworks. In the early 1970s, it was demolished when the whole area was cleared of the old slum housing opposite the vast steelworks, which had also been gone for many years.

By WWII, John was no longer running the Tinsley Hotel and worked as a general labourer. In 1939 War Register, John Edward Banks, born 27 March 1871, a general labourer, at 285 Abbeydale Road, Sheffield, with wife Emma H, born 7 April 1876, an unpaid housekeeper, children Dorothy, born 3 February 1908, a ladies hairdresser, Joseph, born 3 June 1905, a steel erector, and George, born 30 November 1916, a brick setter.

John Edward Banks, 76, died in 1949 (Sheffield, 2D/438) and wife Emma Hetty Banks nee Johnson, 79, died in 1956 (Sheffield, 2D/181).

Gordon's maternal grandparents –
William Edwin Yates and Kate Etherington

Gordon's maternal grandfather William Edwin Yates was born in 1st Quarter 1860 in Nottinghamshire to parents William Yates and Elizabeth Wilson (Worksop, 7B/23).

In 1861, William E, 1, at No.3, Court 2, Worksop, with father William Yates, 37, an agricultural labourer, mother Elizabeth, 33, and brother, John T, 2. In 1871, William E, 11, a scholar, at 33 Abbey Street, Worksop, with father William Yates, 43, a general labourer, mother Elizabeth, 43, a dressmaker, and his siblings.

By 1881, William E Yates, 21, a butcher, lodged at Lord Street, Gainsborough, Lincolnshire, at the home of Peter Cave, 40, a master butcher employing 1 man, William obviously. The butcher shop at No.37 stood next door to Richard A Layne's Tiger Inn, now called Lords, at No.35 Lord Street. It is a Historic England Grade II Listed Building. At No.39 was George Minskip, a fruiterer, and at No.41 was the historic White Lion Inn run by William Harrison, now The Upper Crust Cafe.

His grandmother Kate Etherington was born on 10 June 1866 in Froxfield, Hampshire to parents Elisha Etherington, a carter, and Charlotte Tull (Petersfield, 2C/123). In 1871, Kate, 5, a scholar, in Broadway, Froxfield, with father Elisha Etherington, 33, a carter, mother Charlotte, 31, and her siblings. In 1881, Kate, 14, at Windmill Farm, Barnet, Froxfield, with father Elisha Etherington, 45, an agricultural labourer, mother Charlotte, 41, and her siblings.

William Edwin Yates, 26, married Kate Etherington, 20, in 3rd Quarter 1886 in Hampshire (Petersfield, 2C/239). William and Kate had 9 children, including 8 born in Gainsborough, Lincolnshire; Harry (b. ~1891), George (b. ~1897), Dan (b. ~1899), Doris (b. ~1901), Kitty (b. ~1903), Frank (b. ~1905), Elise (b. ~1908) and Nellie (b. 27 August

1909). Daughter Nellie Yates was born on 27 August 1909 (Gainsborough, 7A/688).

In 1911, William Edwin Yates, 51, a butcher on his own account, at 6 Hooton's Buildings, Gainsborough, with wife Kate, 44, at home, children Harry, 20, boots at a hotel, George, 14, left school, Dan, 12, Doris, 10, Kitty, 8, Frank, 6, all at school, Elise, 3, and Nellie, 1. By 1921, William Edwin Yates, wife Kate, daughter Nellie and 5 other children lived in Sheffield, Yorkshire, where daughter Nellie met future husband Thomas Banks.

William Edwin Yates, 64, died in 1925 (Sheffield, 9C/725) and was buried in Tinsley Park Cemetery. Kate moved back to Lincolnshire and in 1939 War Register, Kate Yates, 73, doing unpaid domestic duties, at 90 Burke Street, Scunthorpe, with Henry Baldwin, 30, an accounts and stock clerk, and wife Valerie, 25. Kate Yates nee Etherington, 79, a widow of 90 Burke Street, Scunthorpe died on 20 July 1946 at 117 Berkeley Street (Scunthorpe, 3B/276). Her estate valued at £403 8s 4d was administered by her daughter Doris Parsons nee Yates.

Gordon's paternal great-grandparents – Thomas Scowcroft Banks and Margaret Hunter

Gordon's paternal great-grandfather Thomas Scowcroft Banks was born around 1839 in Much Hoole village, Lancashire, 6 miles south of Preston, to father John Banks. His great-grandmother Margaret Hunter was also born there around 1838 to father Laurence Hunter. Thomas Banks married his first wife Margaret Wray in 1st Quarter 1858 (Preston, 8E/479). They had a daughter Elizabeth (b. ~1858) in Much Hoole. However, Margaret Banks nee Wray died in early 1859, leaving Thomas a widower. Thomas Scowcroft Banks, an agricultural labourer, married his second wife Margaret Hunter in 2nd Quarter 1859 (Preston, 8E/560).

Thomas and Margaret had 7 known children; in Much Hoole, John (b. ~1860, d. 1 Q. 1863), Laurence (b. ~1865); and in Atherton, Jane (b. ~1867), John Edward (b. 1st Quarter 1873), Mary (b. ~1875), Richard (b. ~1876) and Herbert (b. ~1881). In 1861, Thomas Banks, 21, an agricultural labourer, at the Farm House, Marsh Lane, Much Hoole, Longton, with wife Margaret, 23, daughter Elizabeth, 3, and son John, 1, who died in infancy in 1863. Thomas Scowcroft Banks, only 46, by then an innkeeper, died in 1886 in Atherton (Leigh, 8C/183), leaving his widow Margaret with a large family and to run their hostelry.

In 1891, Margaret Banks, 53, a widowed publican and employer, lived and managed the Punch Bowl Hotel, Atherton, Leigh, with her children Elizabeth, 33, a barmaid, Laurence, 26, a horse dealer, Jane, 24, a barmaid, John E, 17, an assistant employee, Mary, 16, a barmaid, Richard, 15, an errand boy, and Herbert, 10, a scholar. Margaret Banks nee Hunter, 59, an innkeeper, died in 1897 in Atherton (Leigh, 8C/173).

Gordon's maternal great-grandparents – William Yates and Elizabeth Wilson

Gordon's maternal great-grandfather William Yates was born around 1824 in Worksop, Nottinghamshire to father John Yates, a labourer. His great-grandmother Elizabeth Wilson was born in 1828 in Gamston, Nottinghamshire to parents John, a labourer, and Catherine Wilson. Elizabeth was baptized on 20 January 1828 in Gamston by East, Retford.

William Yates, a labourer, who signed with his 'x' mark, married Elizabeth Wilson, both of 'full age', on 24 September 1857 in St Mary and St Cuthbert Priory, Worksop; the best man was Elizabeth's brother Joseph Wilson. William and Kate had 6 known children in Worksop; John Thomas (b. ~1859), William Edwin (b. ~1860), Frank (b. ~1863), Fanny (b. ~1866), Alfred (b. ~1868) and Daniel (b. ~1870).

In 1861, William Yates, 37, an agricultural labourer, at No.3, Court 2, Worksop, with wife Elizabeth, 33, sons John T, 2, and William E, 1. In 1871, William Yates, 43, a general labourer, at 33 Abbey Street, Worksop, with wife Elizabeth, 43, a dressmaker, children John Tom, 12, William E, 11, Frank, 8, Fanny, 5, Alfred, 3, all scholars, and baby Daniel, 1. In 1881, William Yates, 55, a beer-house keeper, at 45 Netherton Road, Worksop, with wife Elizabeth, 53, children John Thomas, 22, a gardener, Fanny, 15, Alfred, 13, and Dan, 11, both at school.

William Yates, 62, died on 23 June 1890 (Worksop, 7B/19) leaving a small estate of £96 11s 6d to his widow Elizabeth. After husband William's death, Elizabeth fell on hard times and she became a pauper. In 1901, Elizabeth Yates, 73, a widowed pauper, resided in the Eastgate Union Workhouse, Worksop. The Worksop Workhouse was built in 1837, however, when Elizabeth was an inmate, it only housed adults. Girls and boys were homed separately in Cheapside. It was demolished in 1965. Elizabeth Yates nee Wilson, 75, still in the Worksop Union Workhouse, died in 1903. She was buried in St Mary & St Cuthbert Priory, Worksop by Rev W W Gawn.

Gordon's maternal great-grandparents – Elisha Etherington and Charlotte Tull

Gordon's other maternal great-grandfather Elisha Etherington aka Elijah was born around 1838 in Hawkley, Hampshire. His great-grandmother Charlotte Tull was born around 1840 in Selbourne, Hampshire. Elisha Etherington, a carter, married Charlotte Tull in 3rd Quarter 1859 in Froxfield, Hampshire (Petersfield, 2C/185). Elisha and Charlotte had 11 known children in Froxfield; Fanny (b. ~1858), Elizabeth (b. ~1860), Emma J (b. ~1862), William (b. ~1864), Kate (b. 2 Q. 1866), George (b. ~1858), Frederick (b. ~1870), Anne (b. ~1873), Mary (b. ~1875), Alice (b. ~1878), Agnes (b. ~1880) and Rose (b. ~1884).

In 1871, Elisha Etherington, 31, a carter, in Broadway, Froxfield with wife Charlotte, 31, children Fanny, 13, an unemployed domestic servant, Elizabeth, 11, Emma J, 9, William, 7, Kate, 5, George, 3, all at school, and Frederick, 1. In 1881, Elisha Etherington, 45, an agricultural labourer, at Windmill Farm, Barnet, Froxfield, with wife Charlotte, 41, children, Kate, 14, George, 12, an agricultural labourer, Frederick, 10, Anne, 8, both scholars, Mary, 6, Alice, 3, and Agnes, 1. In 1901, Elijah Etherington, 62, a farm labourer, at Ragmans Cottage, Froxfield, with wife Charlotte, 60, and daughter Rose, 17, a domestic servant.

Elijah Etherington, 71, died in 1909 and wife Charlotte Etherington nee Tull, 71, died in 1911, both in Petersfield, Hampshire.

CHAPTER 2

George Cohen MBE (right back)

Honours as an England player:
1 FIFA World Cup winner 1966

S even weeks into WWII, George Reginald Cohen MBE was born at 15 Cassidy Road, Fulham, London, on 22 October 1939, to parents Lewis Harry Cohen, a gas fitter, and Catherine Jane Clara Gibbs. His birth was registered in 4th Quarter 1939 (Fulham, 1A/384). Cohen was Fulham through and through. *"I was born in Cassidy Road, right opposite the police station in Fulham Road,"* he once stated. *"I was closer to Stamford Bridge than Craven Cottage but it was easier to bunk into Fulham than it was to get into Chelsea."* According to family legend, Cohen was of Ukrainian Jewish descent on his father's side, however, he was raised in Fulham in the Church of England.

He was an English professional footballer, playing right-back. He spent his entire professional career with Fulham, and won the 1966 World Cup with England. This was the only major football medal Cohen won in his career. He was inducted into the English Football Hall of Fame. He was the uncle of 2003 rugby union World Cup winner Ben Cohen, born in 1978 in Northampton, the son of Cohen's younger brother Peter Cohen.

Cohen was a one-club footballer, joining Fulham in 1956 and remaining there until retirement through injury 13 years later in March 1969. Fulham had been relegated to the Second Division the season before he retired as a player and remained out of the top flight for 33 years. He ended his career with 459 appearances for the club, a figure surpassed by just five other Fulham players. As an attack-minded full-back he scored six league goals for Fulham.

By the time the 1966 World Cup started, Cohen was Alf Ramsey's first choice to replace the injury-prone Blackpool player Jimmy Armfield, who had featured in the 1962 World Cup in Chile. Ramsey's team played without conventional wingers, allowing extra strength in midfield. Instead, they relied on young, stamina-based players like Martin Peters and Alan Ball to drift from centre to flank and back again as required. When these players were occupied in more central positions, or chasing high up the flank and needed support, an attacking full-back like Cohen proved invaluable.

After England's win over Argentina in the quarter-finals, Cohen was photographed in the press depicting a furious Alf Ramsey preventing him from swapping shirts with his Argentine opponent, Alberto Gonzalez. Ramsey later described them as "animals" for their persistent fouling and gamesmanship. Three days later, Cohen's an overlapping run and near-post pass contributed to Bobby Charlton's semi-final clincher as England beat Portugal.

As vice-captain to Bobby Moore in the final against West Germany, Cohen won his 30th cap. He blocked the last-minute Lothar Emmerich free-kick which squirmed across the England six-yard box for Wolfgang Weber to equalise 2–2. England won 4–2 in extra-time. His 37th and final England appearance was a 2–0 win over Northern Ireland at Wembley in 1967.

George's parents –
Lewis Henry Cohen and Catherine Jane Clara Gibbs

George's father Lewis Henry Cohen aka Harry was born on 28 February 1903 in Queen Charlotte's Hospital, Marylebone, London to parents Jacob Solomon Cohen, a house painter's labourer, and Sarah Ann Mann as registered by his mother Sarah Cohen, of 19 Green Street, Chelsea, on 7 March 1903 (Marylebone, 1A/555).

Queen Charlotte's, named after King George III's wife, was originally built as a lying-in hospital for pregnant women. In 1903 it was situated on Marylebone Road, Hammersmith. Then, most births occurred in the home, suggesting Sarah had birth complications with Lewis requiring hospital treatment. As an aside, Dame Helen Mirren (Ilynea Lydia Mirinoff) was born in 1945 in Queen Charlotte's Maternity Hospital and played Queen Charlotte in the film *The Madness of King George*.

Some records state George's mother was born in Ireland, however, this is incorrect. George's mother Catherine Jane Clara Gibbs aka Kate Kathleen was born on 23 September 1909 in Aldershot, Hampshire (Farnham, Surrey, 2A/127). Over a year later, she was baptized as Kathleen Clara Jane Gibbs on 9 February 1911 in Aldershot to parents George Temple Gibbs, a Royal Artillery Gunner, and Jennie Emily Warner. In 1911, 'Katherleen' Gibbs, 2, at 31 Upper William Street, St John's Wood, Marylebone, with her widowed grandmother Sarah Jane Warner, 49, a charwoman, father George Temple Gibbs, 29, an unemployed storeman, mother Jane Emily Warner, 23, a domestic, and two uncles.

In 1921, Lewis Henry Cohen, almost 18½, worked as a hairdresser's porter for Edwin Hill, Court Hairdressers, at 23 Old Bond Street, London. Lewis lived with his siblings and his widowed mother Sarah Cohen, 42, at 35 Denyer Street, Chelsea, London. The street consisted mainly of slum terraced housing. Sarah worked as a saloon cleaner for Robert Douglas, Court Hairdressers, at 21 New Bond Street.

In 1921, Kathleen Gibbs, 12, a scholar, resided in St John's Wood, Marylebone with her mother Jane Gibbs, 33, and younger sister Ellen, 9, a scholar.

Lewis Henry Cohen, 26, a gas fitter, married Kate Gibbs, 23, a restaurant counter hand, both of 3 Adelaide

Place, Adelaide Road, Hampstead, on 11 January 1930 (Hampstead, 1A/1087). The wedding was conducted by E. Best, registrar; the best man was James E Eyres and the best maid was Rose Winifred Manners, Lewis's married sister. Lewis and Kate had 3 known sons in London; Harry Lewis (b. 2 Q. 1930, St George Hanover Square), George Reginald (b. 22 October 1939, Fulham) and Peter J (b. 2 Q. 1942, Fulham).

In 1939 War Register, Lewis H Cohen, born 28 February 1903, a gas fitter, at 15 Cassidy Road, Fulham, with wife Kathleen, born 23 February 1909, doing unpaid domestic duties, and son Harry Lewis, marked as 'record officially closed' due to his young age. Lewis was also acting on civil defence duties for the Gas Light & Coke Company. At that time, Kathleen, also pencilled in as Catherine Jane Clara Gibbs, was pregnant with her son George.

Son George Reginald Cohen was born on 22 October 1939 at 15 Cassidy Road, Fulham to parents Lewis Cohen aka Harry, a gas fitter, and Catherine Gibbs in 4th Quarter 1939 (Fulham, 1A/16). Lewis did not live to see his son George lift the World Cup in 1966. Lewis Henry Cohen, 59, a gas fitter, died in 1963 (Chelsea, 5C/519). His wife Kate Cohen nee Gibbs, 64, died in 1973 (Stepney, 5E/153).

In November 2000, Lewis Cohen's son Peter Cohen, brother of 1966 World Cup winning footballer George Cohen, was fatally injured while protecting an employee under attack. It happened at the Eternity nightclub in Northampton, which he managed. Peter died a month later from head injuries sustained in the assault. Three men were found guilty of violent conduct. Three years later, Peter's son Ben Cohen won the rugby union World Cup in November 2003 with England at Sydney's Stadium Australia. England beat hosts Australia 20–17, won by Jonny Wilkinson's last minute drop goal.

George's paternal grandparents –
Jacob Solomon Cohen and Sarah Ann Mann

George's paternal grandfather Jacob Solomon Cohen aka Jack or Solomon was born around 1878 in Whitechapel, London, to parents Lewis Cohen, a tailor, and Annie Benjamin aka Hannah. Lewis and Annie were born in Poland around 1852–53, in the Russian Empire of Tsar Nikolas I. Family legend believes them to be of Russian Jewish origin from Ukraine, part of Congress Poland. Over a third of Jews in Russian-held Poland lived in Ukraine in the Pale of Settlement.

In 1881, (Jacob) Solomon, 2, at 36 Burne Street, Marylebone, with father Lewis Cohen, 28, a tailor, mother Annie, 29, and his siblings. In 1891, (Jacob) Solomon, 15, at 180 High Holburn, Bloomsbury, London, with father Lewis Cohen, 41, a tailor, mother Annie, 41, and his siblings.

George's grandmother Sarah Ann Mann was born in 2nd Quarter 1878 in London to parents John Thomas Mann and Elizabeth McArthur (Marylebone, 1A/534). In 1881,

Sarah, 3, at 2 Barrett Street, Marylebone, with her father John Mann, 36, a labourer, mother Elizabeth, 38, and her siblings.

Jacob Solomon Cohen, 20, a builder's labourer, of 3 Gray's Yard, Marylebone, married Sarah Ann Mann, 19, of 36 James Street, Marylebone, at the registry office on 26 October 1896 (Marylebone, 1A/1243). The wedding was conducted by Frank Stokes, registrar; the witnesses were John Mann, Louisa Johnson and Lydia Mann. It appears Jacob renounced his Jewish faith at the marriage.

Jacob and Sarah had 4 known children; Dora (b. 28 July 1899, Marylebone), Lewis Henry aka Harry (b. 28 February 1903), Rose Winifred aka Freda (b. ~1905, Chelsea) and Leonard aka Lennie (b. ~1908, Chelsea). Daughter Dora Cohen was born on 28 July 1899 at 13 Gees Court, Oxford Street, London, to parents Jacob Solomon Cohen, a labourer, and Sarah Mann. Dora was baptized on 31 July 1899 by Rev G C Campbell.

In 1901, Jacob S Cohen, 22, a miller's chaff cutter, at 24 Little Marylebone Street, Marylebone, with wife Sarah, 23, and daughter Dora, 1. A chaff cutting machine, which Jacob operated, is a mechanical device for cutting and milling hay and straw into small pieces for mixing into animal forage. Son Lewis Henry Cohen aka Harry was born on 28 February 1903 in Queen Charlotte's Hospital, Marylebone to parents Jacob Solomon Cohen, a house painter's labourer, and Sarah Mann. He was registered by his mother Sarah Cohen on 7 March 1903 (Marylebone, 1A/555). Sarah recorded the family living in Chelsea, probably 19 Green Street, as they lived there when son Leonard was baptized at St Saviour's Church, Upper Chelsea.

In 1911, (Jacob) Solomon Cohen, 33, a painter's labourer for a builder, at 19 Green Street, Chelsea with wife Sarah, 33, children Dora, 11, Lewis (stated erroneously as George), 8, Rose Winifred, 5, all at school, and Leonard, 2½. The likelihood is the Cohen's were decanted soon after as the Duke of Westminster instructed the erection of new Palladian buildings between 1912–14 and Green Street, once known as Green Lettuce Lane, is now in upmarket Mayfair, near Marble Arch.

Jacob Solomon Cohen, only 37, died in 1914 (Chelsea, 1A/409), leaving Sarah widowed with young children. In 1921, widowed Sarah Cohen, 42, a saloon cleaner for Robert Douglas, Court Hairdressers, 21 New Bond Street, at 35 Denyer Street, Chelsea, with children Dora, 22, a hairdresser's saloon attendant for Robert Douglas, Lewis Henry, almost 18½, a hairdresser's porter for Edwin Hill, Court Hairdressers, 23 Old Bond Street, Rose Winifred, almost 16, assistant waitress for E Splues, fancy baker and tea shop, and Leonard, 13, at school.

The term 'court hairdressers' developed from 18th century hair salons providing wig styling services to the courtiers and servants of the Royal Court. However, not to the Royal Family, who had their own private stylists. Court hairdressers started out providing powdered wigs, oils and scents, when they were the fashion at Court. Now trading as Truefitt & Hill in St James's Street, London by Royal

Warrant from King George III, it is in the Guinness Book of World Records as the oldest barbershop in the world.

George's maternal grandparents –
George Temple Gibbs and Jane Emily Warner

George's maternal grandfather George Temple Gibbs was born around 1882 in Fort George Barracks, St Peter Port, Guernsey, Channel Islands, to parents George Henry Gibbs, a Royal Artillery Gunner, and Clara Hancox Patston. In 1891, George, 9, a scholar, at 46 Ordnance Road, Woolwich, with father George Gibbs, 40, a servant at the Royal Military Academy, Woolwich, mother Clara, 31, brothers Alfred, 11, a scholar, and Arthur, 1 month old.

George's maternal grandmother Jane Emily Warner aka Jennie was born in 2nd Quarter 1888 at 27 Barrow Hill Road, St John's Wood, London to parents John William Warner, a carman, and Sarah Jane Veale (Marylebone, 1A/623), baptized 6 May 1888 in St Stephen the Martyr, Hampstead. In 1901, Jane E, 13, a scholar, resided in Upper William Street, St John's Wood, Marylebone, with father John W Warner, 35, a builder's carman, mother Sarah Jane, and her siblings.

Attested in the British Army on 7 November 1897, George Temple Gibbs served as a Gunner, Royal Artillery in the South Africa Campaign from 1899 to 1902. For his service in the Boer War, he was awarded Queen Victoria's South Africa Medal 1899, with clasps for Cape Colony, Orange

Free State, Transvaal, He also received the South Africa Medals for 1901 and 1902.

Back home, George passed the First Aid to the wounded class of instruction on 5 June 1903. He received a 3rd Class Certificate of Education on 21 September 1904. On 19 May 1905, George received a severe wound to his left shin while on active service with the Royal Horse Artillery stationed in Lucknow, India. In 1905, on Hart's annual army list, 'O' Battery RHA was stationed in Lucknow commanded by Major A H Hussey.

George served in 'A' Battery RHA in 1908 and 1909. On paid leave, George Temple Gibbs, Gunner 24001, Royal Horse Artillery, married Jane Emily Warner on 30 October 1908, in Marylebone Register Office. They had a daughter Catherine Jane Clara Gibbs born on 23 February 1909 in Aldershot (Farnham, 2A/127) and baptized on 9 February 1911. In 1909, George was transferred as a Gunner from the RHA to the Royal Artillery Army Reserve at Aldershot. He remained in reserve from 1909 until the outbreak of WWI.

In 1911, after two years of marriage, George Temple Gibbs, 29, an unemployed storeman, at 31 Upper William Street, St John's Wood, Marylebone, with wife Jane Emily Warner, 23, a domestic, his daughter 'Katherleen', 2, his widowed mother-in-law Sarah Jane Warner, 49, a char-woman, brother-in-law Henry Warner, 17, a grocer's assistant carman, Alfred Warner, 10, a schoolboy, and lodger Joseph Dixon, 17, a watchmaker's general assistant.

Daughter Ellen Florence Martha Gibbs was born in 3rd Quarter 1912 to parents George Temple Gibbs, a porter, and

Jane Emily Warner, both of 4 Lancaster Mews, Hampstead (Marylebone, 1A/1037), baptized on 1 September 1912 at St Stephen the Martyr, Hampstead. In 1913 Electoral Register for London, George Temple Gibbs was a registered voter at 2 Llanover Road, Woolwich. In 1915 Electoral Register for London, George Temple Gibbs was a registered voter at 26 Henry Street, Marylebone, and also 3 Eland Road, Woolwich.

As an ex-serving professional soldier on the Army Reserve, George Temple Gibbs, 27, of 9 Brighton Road, Aldershot, was re-mobilized at Woolwich Barracks for war service on 5 August 1914. He served in the Royal Artillery. George, a labourer by trade, was described as a tall soldier at 5 feet 10 inches, with a fresh complexion, blue eyes and brown hair. He served with the British Expeditionary Forces in France between 1914 and 1915, having arrived in France on 5 November 1914. On 29 July 1917, in a prelude to the Battle of Passchendaele, after a furious artillery barrage near Lens in Flanders, George suffered multiple contusions. The contusions were described as 'trivial' by the army surgeon. At that time, wife Jane and daughter Katherine lived at 9 Brighton Road, near Aldershot Park.

After recovering from his wounds, George, a Gunner, left France on 9 January 1918. He was attached back in England to the RA Command Depot, Ripon, Yorkshire, from 13 February 1918 until 22 June 1918. He was transferred to Bedford Regimental Depot on 16 August 1918. As the war ended, George was permanently and compulsorily trans-ferred to Private 665055, Corps A32 Agricultural Company,

Labour Corps, Bedford. This suggests he was physically unfit to return to the front as a fighting soldier and was employed in agricultural work. For his service in WWI, George was awarded the 1915 Star, the British War and Victory Medals.

In 1921, Jane Gibbs, 33, resided in St John's Wood, Marylebone with daughters Kathleen, 12, and Ellen, 9, both scholars. George was on attachment to the army in Somerset. On 11 February 1926, George Temple Gibbs, 42, a porter from 43 Cochrane Street, St Johns Wood, was set to sail to Sydney, Australia on Ticket No.1755 aboard the P&O Lines SS 'Berrima'. However, his name was struck out, possibly as a result of illness. George never sailed to Australia and the following year, George Temple Gibbs, only 45, a school porter, died in 3rd Quarter 1927 (Marylebone, 1A/494). George was buried on 6 September 1927 in Hendon Cemetery, Barnet. Jane Emily Gibbs nee Warner, 68, died in 3rd Quarter 1956 (Paddington, 5D/164). Jane was buried on 12 November 1956 in Kensington and Chelsea Cemetery.

George's paternal great-grandparents – Lewis Cohen and Hannah Benjamin

George's paternal great-grandfather Lewis Cohen was born around 1853. Huge numbers of Jews adopted the surname Cohen, from 'kohen' meaning a priest in Hebrew, to avoid conscription into the Russian army. George's great-grandmother Hannah Benjamin aka Annie was born around 1852 to parents Simeon aka Simon and Dora Benjamin. They were all born in Congress Poland, Tsarist Russia, according to family legend in Ukraine. The Pale of Settlement was a huge swathe of the Russian Empire stretching from Lithuania in the north to Ukraine and Crimea in the south. Outside the Pale, most Jews were forbidden to live elsewhere in the Russian Empire.

Even within the Pale, Jews were forced to live in crowded ghettos and subjected to violent pogroms. During the 19th century hundreds of thousands of Russian Jews emigrated west. Many migrated to Western Poland and Germany and found their descendants caught up in WWII's Nazi Holocaust. In January 1863, a major uprising began in Krakow, fought by 'White partisans', which was quelled by Tsarist forces in spring 1864. It is uncertain where Lewis originated, possibly from Ukraine, but Hannah's origins are clear.

Simeon and Dora Benjamin were born around 1831 in the historic provincial capital city of Plock (Plotsk in Yiddish), Mazowiecke, Congress Poland, 72 miles west of Warsaw. Daughter Hannah Benjamin was born there around 1852. The Krakow Uprising spread to Plock and the rebel leader, Zygmunt Padlewski, was executed there by the Russians in May 1863. Many Jews fled Poland fearing further reprisals, including Lewis and Hannah.

In 1871, Lewis Cohen, 17, a tailor, boarded at 1 Marlborough Court, Petticoat Lane, Whitechapel, the home of Benjamin Woolf, 41, a Hebrew teacher. In 1871, Hannah, 18, a tailoress, at No.2 Parliament Court, Old

Artillery Ground, Whitechapel, with father Simeon Benjamin, 40, a zinc worker, mother Dora, 40, siblings Fanny, 16, Betsy, 14, also tailoresses, Jane, 12, Harris, 9, Gershon, 7, and Morris, 4. Parliament Court is now bricked up at 1a Sandys Row. At No.5, the Parliament Court Chapel was built by French Huguenots in 1766. Dutch Ashkenazi Jews consecrated it as Sandys Row Synagogue on 6 November 1870. The Old Artillery Ground got its name from the historic firing range for Henry VIII's Royal Artillery.

Lewis Cohen married Hannah Benjamin in 3rd Quarter 1872 (London City, 1C/208). Lewis and Hannah had 4 known children; Abraham (b. ~1876, Whitechapel), Jacob Solomon (b. ~1878, Whitechapel), Dora Winifred (b. ~1880, Marylebone) and Ada (b. ~1883, Paddington). In 1881, Lewis Cohen, 28, a tailor, at 36 Burne Street, Marylebone, with wife Annie, 29, brother-in-law Maurice Benjamin, 14, children Abraham, 5, (Jacob) Solomon Cohen, 2, and Dora F, 4 months old.

In 1881, Simon and Dora Benjamin at 82 Plumbers Row, Whitechapel. Simon and Dora do not appear in the Sandys Row Synagogue records. They probably attended Polish Synagogue at on Cutler Street. By 1891 they were still there; Simon Benjamin, 50, a plumber's gas fitter, with wife Dora, 56, and son Maurice, 24, a furrier, all born in Plotsk, Poland. This was the infamous period when Jack the Ripper murdered Victorian prostitutes in Whitechapel, with some xenophobic periodicals purporting the serial killer to be Jewish or foreign. Dora Benjamin, 67, died in 1900 and

Simon Benjamin, 65, a gasfitter, died in 1903 at 8 Fieldgate Street, Whitechapel.

From 1884 to 1891, on the ledgers for Sandys Row Synagogue, Lewis Cohen paid between 2 and 6 shillings. In 1891, Lewis Cohen, 41, a tailor, at 180 High Holborn, Bloomsbury, London, with wife Annie, 41, children Abraham, 16, (Jacob) Solomon, 15, Dora, 10, and Ada, 6. In 1892, Lewis paid 3 shillings. In 1896 he was listed as seat holder No.35 at Sandys Row Synagogue. He was issued receipt No.178 for 3 shillings on 6 September 1896.

In 1901, Lewis Cohen, 50, a hosier on his own account, at 1 Iffley Road, Fulham, with wife Annie, 50, daughter Ada, 17, and grandson Joseph, 5. Lewis Cohen was dead by 1911, when Hannah Cohen, 62, a widow, at 434 Hackney Road, Bethnal Green, with son-in-law Isaac Hershon, 27, a boot manufacturer's finisher, and recently married daughter Ada Hershon, 27. Ada Hershon, 35, died on 2 October 1918 and buried in plot L/10/41 in Edmonton Federation Cemetery. Hannah Cohen, 75, died in 1926 in Hackney.

George's paternal great-grandparents – John Thomas Mann and Elizabeth McArthur

George's other paternal great-grandfather John Thomas Mann was born around 1838 and his great-grandmother Elizabeth McArthur (or MacArthur) was born around 1843, both in Marylebone, London. John Thomas Mann married Elizabeth McArthur on 30 July 1866 (Marylebone, 1A/962). John and Elizabeth posted their Banns of marriage on three consecutive Sabbaths; 15, 22 and 29 July 1866 in Christ Church, Marylebone. They were married on Monday 30 July 1866 in Christ Church. John and Elizabeth had 8 known children in Marylebone; Frederick (b. 3 Q. 1865, illegitimate), John (b. ~1868), Emily (b. ~1870), Louisa (b. ~1871), Elizabeth (b. ~1873), Mary (b. ~1876), Sarah Ann (b. 2 Q. 1878) and Ellen (b. ~1880). Daughter Sarah Ann Mann was born in 2nd Quarter 1878 (Marylebone, 1A/534).

In 1881, John Mann, 36, a labourer, at 2 Barrett Street, Marylebone, with wife Elizabeth, 38, children Emily, 11, Louisa, 10, Elizabeth, 8, Mary, 5, all at school, Sarah, 3, and Ellen, 1. In 1891, John Mann, 53, a bricklayer, at 30 James Street, Marylebone, with wife Elizabeth, 38, a tailoress, children Frederick, 26, a painter, John, 23, a labourer, Elizabeth, 17, a general servant, Mary, 15, a housemaid, Sarah, 14, and Ellen, 10. In 1901, John Mann, 65, a bricklayer, still resided there with wife Elizabeth, 57, a tailoress, and daughter Mary, 23, a dressmaker. John Mann, 65, died in 1903 in Chelsea and his wife Elizabeth Mann nee McArthur died in 1915 in Willesden.

George's maternal great-grandparents –
John William Warner and Sarah Jane Veale

George's maternal great-grandfather John William Warner was born in 3rd Quarter 1866 in London to parents John and Mary Ann Warner (Marylebone, 1A/528). In 1871, John W, 5, at 23 Upper William Street, Marylebone, with father John Warner, 30, a coachman, (b. ~1841, Hendon, Middlesex) mother Mary Ann, 26, a charwoman, (b. ~1845, Marylebone), sister Mary Ann, 6, and brother Edward G, 2.

George's maternal great-grandmother Sarah Jane Veale was born on 9 July 1863 in Pimlico, London to parents Robert Cotton Veale (b. ~1821, Bristol) and Jane Ash (b. ~1822, Edington, Somerset). Robert Cotton Veale married Jane Ash in 1st Quarter 1858 (Marylebone, 1A/538). Sarah Jane Veale was baptized on 2 August 1863 in St Peter's Church, Eaton Square, Pimlico. In 1871, Sarah Jane, 8, at 9 Alexander Mews, St John's, Hampstead, with father Robert C Veale, 32, a smith and farrier, mother Jane, 35, and brother Robert, 9, (b. ~1862, Pimlico). In 1881, Sarah Jane Veale, 19, a general servant, resided below stairs at Draycott House, Horn Lane, West Acton, Middlesex, at the home of Walter Adam Brown, 42, a solicitor. Draycott House was demolished in 1899. The *London Standard* reported on 9 August 1899 that a valuable plot of land was secured for sale at Highfield Elm Bank, Langley Villa and Draycott House.

John William Warner married Sarah Jane Veale in 2nd Quarter 1887 (Marylebone, 1A/1066). John and Sarah had 9 known children in St John's Wood, Marylebone; Jane

Emily (b. 2 Q 1888), Florence Martha (b. 5 June 1889), Robert J (b. ~1890, died in infancy), George E (b. ~1891), Henry A (b. ~1894), Ellen A (b. ~1895), Martha (b. ~1897), John (b. ~1899) and Alfred C (b. ~1901).

In 1891, John William Warner, 26, a grocer's carman, resided in Henry Street, Marylebone, with wife Sarah J, 27, Jane E, 3, Florence M, 2, and baby Robert J. In 1901, John W Warner, 35, a builder's carman, at 31 Upper William Street, St John's Wood, Marylebone, with wife Sarah Jane, 34, children Jane E, 13, Florence M, 12, George E, 10, Henry A, 7, Ellen A, 6, Martha, 4, John, 2, and baby Alfred C. John William Warner, only 42, of 31 Upper William Street, Marylebone, died in December 1908 and was buried on 2 January 1909 in Hendon Cemetery, Barnet, presided over by Rev J W Wilson, and undertaker was A G Hurry of St John's Wood.

In 1911, widowed Sarah Jane Warner, 49, a charwoman, at 31 Upper William Street, St John's Wood, Marylebone, with son-in-law George Temple Gibbs, 29, an unemployed storeman, daughter Jane Emily Warner, 23, a domestic, granddaughter 'Katherleen', 2, sons Henry Warner, 17, a grocer's assistant carman, Alfred Warner, 10, a schoolboy, and lodger Joseph Dixon, 17, a watchmaker's general assistant. On 26 January 1913, Sarah's daughter Florence Martha Warner, 23, of 36 Henry Street, Marylebone, married John Coombes, 28, a Gunner, Royal Horse Artillery, based at St John's Wood Barracks, Ordnance Road, Woolwich, in St Stephen the Martyr Church; sister Ellen Warner was the best maid. Florence's father was John William Warner, a carman, deceased. Sarah Jane Warner nee Veale, 75, died in 1938 in Grantham, Lincolnshire.

George's maternal great-grandparents –
George Henry Gibbs and Clara Hancox Patston

George's other maternal great-grandfather George Henry Gibbs was born in 3rd Quarter 1850 in Solihull, Warwickshire, to father John Gibbs, a farmer. His great-grandmother Clara Hancox Patston was born around 1859 in Birmingham, Warwickshire to father John Patston, a pearl worker. In the 19th century, Birmingham was famed for its pearl workers, known as the 'pearlies'. Pearl workers were employed in various businesses mainly in Birmingham's historic Jewellery Quarter. They produced fashionable pearl buttons from exotic shells, but also more upmarket pearl necklaces.

In 1871, George Gibbs was a Gunner in the Royal Horse Artillery based at Cavalry Barracks, Birmingham. The Cavalry Barracks were also known as Duddeston Barracks in Great Brook Street. They were built in 1793 for cavalry regiments to quell anti-monarchy riots, however, from the 1870s they were used by the Royal Horse Artillery. George Henry Gibbs, 29, a soldier, married Clara Hancox Patston, 21, both of Park Road, Birmingham, on 1 March 1881 in All Saints Church, Birmingham; the witnesses were John Patston and Catherine Patston. George and Clara had 6 known children; Alfred (b. ~1881, Portsmouth), George Temple (b. ~1882, Guernsey), Arthur (b. ~1891, Woolwich, died in infancy),

John (b. ~1896, Woolwich), Henry (b. ~1897, Woolwich), Clara Frances (b. ~1899, died shortly after birth).

In 1881, George was stationed at the Royal Field Artillery Barracks at Hilsea, Portsmouth, where his son Alfred was born. Hilsea Barracks was constructed in 1780 for Portsmouth Dockyards defence from French invasion. When George arrived in 1881, there were three long brick-built barracks surrounding the parade ground, with officers stationed in Gatcombe House. There was room for two batteries of artillerymen, their horses and gun carriages.

It is likely George's battery was bound for Guernsey in the Channel Islands. The following year in 1882, George was stationed at Fort George, St Peter Port, Guernsey. George and Clara's son George Temple Gibbs was born there that year. Fort George was planned for the Channel Islands defence following the Battle of Jersey in 1781 against French and American Revolutionary forces. The star-shaped fort, replacing Castle Cornet, was completed in 1812 to deter French invasion under Napoleon Bonaparte. The fort attracted dubious activities in the many nearby 'maisons de débauche'. Bye-laws of 1895 and 1912 were enforced to deport foreign women employed in prostitution.

In 1891, George Gibbs, 40, a servant at the Royal Military Academy, Woolwich, at 46 Ordnance Road, Woolwich, with wife Clara, 31, sons Alfred, 11, George, 9, both scholars, and Arthur, 1 month old. The Royal Academy in Woolwich was a military training school for commissioned officers in the Royal Artillery and Royal Engineers. After George's soldiering career ended he took a job attending to officer cadets.

Clara Gibbs, only 40, died in spring 1899 in Woolwich after giving birth to daughter Clara Frances Gibbs, who also died shortly after birth. In 1901, widowed George H Gibbs, 48, a servant at the Royal Military Academy, Woolwich, still at 46 Ordnance Road, Woolwich, with sons John, 5, and Henry, 4. George Henry Gibbs, only 52, died in 1904 in Woolwich.

CHAPTER 3

Ray Wilson MBE (left back)

Honours as an England player:
1 FIFA World Cup 1966

Ramon Wilson MBE, aka Ray, was born on 17 December 1934 in Shirebrook, Derbyshire to parents William Henry Wilson and Elizabeth Mason (Mansfield, 7B/135). In 1939 War Register, when Ray was age 4, the Wilson family at 43 Ridgeway, Blackwell, Bolsover, Derbyshire. Ray was an English professional footballer who played left back. He was a member of the England national team that won the 1966 World Cup. After leaving school in 1948, Wilson became an apprentice railwayman on the recently nationalized British Railways. However, he was spotted by a scout playing amateur football at Huddersfield Town. He began working on the railway tracks by night and training with Huddersfield by day, before being called up for national service.

Quickly singled out as a strong, nippy left back, with good overlapping skills by Huddersfield Town manager Bill Shankly, Wilson signed professional forms with the club in 1952 and after his two-year army posting, he made his debut against Manchester United in October 1955. Two years later, Wilson was Huddersfield's first-choice left back. He moved to Everton in 1964, winning the FA Cup with the Toffees in that historic year of 1966. He later moved to Oldham Athletic in 1969, finally transferring to Bradford City in 1970.

Wilson, who played in the 1962 World Cup in Chile, was the oldest member of the England team in the 1966 World Cup final against West Germany. His early headed clearance fell to striker Helmut Haller, who gave the Germans the lead as a result. However, after a hat-trick from Geoff Hurst, England ran out 4–2 winners. After retiring from football, Wilson set up an undertaker's business in Huddersfield.

Ray's parents –
William Henry Wilson and Elizabeth Mason

Ray's father William Henry Wilson was born on 23 February 1901 in Hanley, Staffordshire, to parents Noah Wilson, a miner, and Lydia Steventon (or Stevens) (Stoke-on-Trent, 6B/220). In 1901, William Henry, 1 month old, at 146 Sun Street, Hanley, Stoke-on-Trent, with father Noah Wilson, 22, a collier loader and hewer, and mother Lydia, 22. In

1911, William Henry, 10, a scholar, at 83 Portland Road, Shirebrook, Mansfield, with father Noah Wilson, 32, a coal miner hewer, mother Lydia, 32, and his siblings.

Too young to fight during WWI, William Henry Wilson, 18, a miner, son of Mrs Wilson, 83 Portland Road, Shirebrook, Derbyshire, enlisted in June 1919 at Clipstone, Nottinghamshire as Gunner 285184 (later 1035658) in the Royal Artillery, initially posted to 1A Reserve Brigade. On 18 June 1919, William was posted to 3rd Brigade, J Battery, Royal Horse Artillery. He was discharged on 21 December 1920, his character described as 'very good'.

Ray's mother Elizabeth Mason aka Lizzie was born in Shirebrook, Derbyshire on 18 May 1902 to parents Herbert Mason and Alice Berridge (Mansfield, 7B/84). In 1911, Elizabeth, 8, at school, at 3 Market Street, Shirebrook, with father Herbert Mason, 36, a coal miner, mother Alice, 37, and her siblings.

William Henry Wilson married Elizabeth Mason in 3rd Quarter 1922 (Mansfield, 7B/339). William and Elizabeth had 4 known children in Shirebrook; William (b. 1 Q. 1923), Doris (b. 1 Q. 1924), Herbert (b. 13 March 1925) and Ramon aka Ray (b. 17 December 1934). Son Ramon Wilson was born on 17 December 1934 in Shirebrook, Derbyshire (Mansfield, 7B/135).

In 1939 War Register, William H Wilson, born 23 February 1901, a colliery ripper doing heavy work, at 43 Ridgeway, Blackwell, Bolsover, Derbyshire, with wife Elizabeth, born 18 May 1902, doing unpaid domestic duties, and son Herbert, born 13 March 1925, a colliery haulage hand. Son Ramon is almost certainly at home, marked 'record officially closed' due to his young age. Also living there were Elizabeth's brothers Henry Mason, born 25 July 1905, a railway wagon builder and repairer, and Eric Mason, born 11 April 1916, a railway wagon repairer.

Elizabeth Wilson nee Mason, only 48, died in 1950 in Mansfield, Nottinghamshire and her husband William Henry Wilson, 70, died in 1971 in Chesterfield, Derbyshire.

Ray's paternal grandparents –
Noah Wilson and Lydia Ellen Steventon

Ray's paternal grandfather Noah Wilson was born around 1878 in Hanley, Stoke-on-Trent, Staffordshire, to parents John Wilson and Jane Ellen Jones. In 1891, Noah, 13, at 91 Bridge Street, Stoke-on-Trent, with father John Wilson, 44, an iron worker, mother Jane, 39, and his siblings.

His grandmother Lydia Ellen Steventon (or Stevens) was born in 4th Quarter 1879 in Hanley to parents John Steventon aka James and Lydia Whitehouse (Stoke-on-Trent, 6B/251). In 1891, Lydia, 12, at home, at 67 Hicken's Row, Stoke-on-Trent, with father James Steventon, 55, a forge labourer, mother Lydia, 49, and her 3 sisters.

Noah Wilson, 20, married Lydia Stevens, 20, both of 67 Ikin's Row, Shelton, on 18 September 1899 in St Mark's Church, Shelton (Stoke-on-Trent, 6B/380). Noah and

Lydia had 10 known children, although 1 died in infancy; in Hanley, Ethel (b. ~1899, illegitimate), William Henry (b. 23 February 1901); in Warsop, Nellie (b. 11 February 1903); in Shirebrook, Elsie May (b. 14 January 1905), Jane (b. 22 December 1906), Lydia (b. 5 September 1909), Joseph (b. 16 December 1911), John (b. 29 April 1913) and Henry (b. 15 March 1915). Daughter Ethel Wilson was baptized on 14 March 1900 at St Mark's, Shelton, Stoke-on-Trent. Son William Henry Wilson was born on 23 February 1901 in Hanley (Stoke-on-Trent, 6B/220).

In 1901, Noah Wilson, 22, a collier loader and hewer, at 146 Sun Street, Hanley, Stoke-on-Trent, with wife Lydia, 22, and son William Henry, 1 month old. In 1911, Noah Wilson, 32, a coal miner hewer, at 83 Portland Road, Shirebrook, Mansfield, with wife Lydia, 32, children Ethel, 11, William Henry, 10, Nellie, 8, Elsie May, 6, Jane, 4, Lydia, 1, and baby Joseph. Also visiting was brother-in-law Edward Jones, 36, a miner loader, and wife Sarah, 30.

Noah Wilson, almost 37, a miner at Warsop Main Colliery for 8 years, of 83 Portland Road, Shirebrook, enlisted at Chesterfield on 6 April 1915 as Private 18650 (later 19149) 13th Lancashire Fusiliers. On 2 September 1915, Noah was transferred to 10th Lancashire Fusiliers, British Expeditionary Force, landing at Boulogne, France. He joined the regiment in the Ypres Salient in Flanders conducting defensive trench warfare, strategically significant for the BEF. If Ypres fell the Germans would break through to the Channel ports. BEF Commander at Ypres, General Sir John French launched an attack towards the German lines at Menin on 19 October 1915. However, General von Falkenhayn launched a counter-offensive the following day, and Noah sustained a disabling injury during the battle, which ultimately ended in a stalemate.

On 29 December 1915, the Army Pay Office, Preston received the following verbatim letter from Lydia Wilson:-

> *Mrs N Wilson, 83 Portland Road, Shirebrook, nr. Mansfield (stamped 1463):*
> *Dear Sir, would you be so kind has to lit me know the where abouts of Pte Noah Wilson my Husband, he is in the 10th Lanc. Fus. and his number is 19149 and the last I heard from him was five weeks agoe when he was in the hospital but were I don't know and I have wrote to the War Office and I have had no answer yet and I am much trubeled about him and I would be very glad if you could let me know something about him, and he is in 2 Coy, from Mrs Wilson.*

After a spell in hospital in France, with a further spell in the Western General Hospital, Manchester, Noah returned to Depot Barracks on 23 May 1916. His army character was described as 'a steady, well behaved man'.

He was discharged from active duty on 23 November 1916. Noah applied for a Chelsea Pension, due to the disability received while on active duty with the BEF. He received the Silver War Badge on 6 January 1917 which was posted to 83 Portland Road. He was officially demobbed on 3 October 1919 and on 13 December 1921. Noah acknowledged receipt of 1914-15 Star, British War and Victory Medals, issued from Fulwood Barracks, Preston.

Noah returned to light colliery work with the Markham & Staveley Coal & Iron Company at Warsop Main colliery in the Nottinghamshire coalfields. Noah Wilson, 57, died in 1936 in Shirebrook (Mansfield, 7B/94). Lydia Wilson nee Steventon, 86, died in 1965 (Chesterfield, Derbyshire, 3A/160).

Ray's maternal grandparents –
Herbert Mason and Alice Berridge

Ray's maternal grandfather Herbert Mason was born on 27 September 1874 in Langwith, Derbyshire to parents Thomas Mason, a horse keeper, and Ann Newcombe. In 1881, Herbert, 6, a scholar, resided in Bolsover, Derbyshire, with father Thomas Mason, 47, a colliery horse keeper, mother Ann, 45, and his siblings. In 1891, Herbert, 16, an apprentice, at 46 Newgate Lane, Mansfield, Nottinghamshire, with father Thomas Mason, 58, an ostler groom, mother Ann, 55, and his brother Charles, 18, an apprentice.

Ray's grandmother Alice Berridge was born in 1st Quarter 1874 in Nottinghamshire to parents Frederick Berridge and Elizabeth Espley (Mansfield, 7B/88). In 1881, Alice, 7, a scholar, at 1 Bowmar Court, Mansfield, with father Frederick Berridge, 45, a wood turner, mother Elizabeth, 46, and her siblings. In 1891, Alice, 17, a doubler at a cotton mill, at 2 Nottingham Road, Mansfield with father

Frederick Berridge, 55, a wood turner, mother Elizabeth, 56, and his sister Elizabeth, 10, a scholar.

Herbert Mason married Alice Berridge in 2nd Quarter 1895 (Mansfield, 7B/106). Herbert and Alice had 11 known children, although 3 died in infancy before 1911. The surviving children were Charles Frederick aka Fred (b. ~1897, Pontefract), Alice Annie (b. ~1899, Mansfield); in Shirebrook, Elizabeth (b. 5 June 1902), Henry (b. 25 July 1905), Herbert (b. ~1908), Ada (b. ~1910), Elsie (b. 3 Q. 1913) and Eric (b. 11 April 1916). Daughter Elizabeth Mason was born on 5 June 1902 in Shirebrook, Derbyshire to parents Herbert Mason and Alice Berridge (Mansfield, 7B/84).

In 1911, Herbert Mason, 36, a coal miner, at 3 Market Street, Shirebrook, with wife Alice, 37, children Fred, 14, at the colliery pit bank, Alice Annie, 12, Elizabeth, 8, Henry, 6, Herbert, 3, all at school, and Ada, 9 months old. Herbert also had a boarder George William Mason, 30, a coal miner hewer, most likely a relative.

Son Charles Frederick Mason, a coal miner, enlisted on 9 December 1915, in WWI, at Derby as Private 117250 in the 13th Sherwood Foresters. Charles served, before the war, in the territorials with the 3rd Leicestershire. Charles was recorded as 5 foot 8½ inches tall, chest girth 36 inches, of good physical development and of good character. He had a tattoo of 'Clara' on his left arm. He cited his father Herbert Mason of 3 Market Street, Shirebrook, Mansfield as his next of kin.

He was transferred as Private 54351 to the Royal Warwickshire Regiment, where he served in the Italian

Campaign. He was issued with a rifle, sword-bayonet and scabbard, complete equipment according to unit, entrenching equipment, a steel helmet, great coat, box respirator and Army Book 64.

At the Battle of Asiago on 15–16 June 1918, the Royal Warwickshire regiment held the left flank facing the Austro-Hungarian forces. The enemy attack was repelled and this was the last time British forces faced an Austrian offensive. The enemy were effectively in retreat from this point onwards. The Austrians were finally defeated by the Italians at the Battle of Vittorio Veneto on 24 October 1918. Charles was demobbed on 9 February 1919 and awarded the British War and Victory Medals.

Alice Mason nee Berridge, 58, died in 1932 (Mansfield, 7B/77). In 1939 War Register, widowed Herbert Mason, born 27 September 1874, an underground colliery stone worker, at 3 Market Street, Blackwell, Bolsover. Herbert Mason, 69, died in 1944 in Chesterfield, Derbyshire.

Ray's paternal great-grandparents – John Wilson and Jane Ellen Jones

Ray's paternal great-grandfather John Wilson was born around 1848 in Dawley Magna, Wellington, Shropshire, to parents Joseph and Mary Wilson. He was baptized there on 13 February 1848. In 1861, John, 14, a mill man, in Horsehay, Dawley, with father Joseph Wilson, 39, an iron puddler (b. ~1822, Dawley), mother Mary, 39, (b. ~1822, Wellington), siblings Benjamin, 15, a forge man, Rebecca, 9, a scholar, Noah, 3, and a cousin Samuel Cotton, 7.

His great-grandmother Jane Ellen Jones was born in 1st Quarter 1854 in Wellington, Shropshire to father William Jones. Jane's birth mother was dead before 1871. In 1871, Jane E, 17, a domestic servant, in Old Park, Dawley, with father William Jones, 43, a pit sinker, stepmother Mary, 44, brother John, 19, a collier, step-siblings Sarah A Bailey, 20, a domestic servant, Eliza Bailey, 17, a seamstress picker, and Thomas, 8, a scholar. John and Jane had 6 known children; in Wellington, John (b. ~1873, illegitimate); in Hanley, Stoke-on-Trent, Mary (b. ~1874), Joseph (b. ~1876), Noah (b. ~1878), James (b. ~1882) and William Henry (b. ~1885).

In 1881, John Wilson, 30, an iron worker, at 113 Tramway, Hanley, Stoke-on-Trent, with wife Jane, 27, children John, 8, Mary, 6, and Joseph, 4. In 1891, John Wilson, 44, an iron worker, at 91 Bridge Street, Stoke-on-Trent, with wife Jane, 39, children John, 19, an iron worker, Mary, 17, a tile maker, Joseph, 15, an iron worker, Noah, 13, James, 7, and William, 2. In 1901, John Wilson, 57, a forge ironworker, was still there with wife Jane, 52, sons James, 19, a miner loader, and William Henry, 16, an underground miner horse driver.

Ray's paternal great-grandparents –
John Steventon and Lydia Whitehouse

Ray's other paternal great-grandfather John Steventon (or Stevens or Stevenson) aka James was born in 1837 in West Bromwich, Staffordshire to parents William and Hannah Steventon, baptized on 26 February 1837 at St Thomas Church, Dudley. His great-grandmother Lydia Whitehouse was born on 9 January 1840 in Dudley, Staffordshire to parents William and Sarah Whitehouse. Lydia was baptized on 18 April 1841 at St Thomas Church, Dudley.

John Steventon married Lydia Whitehouse in 3rd Quarter 1858 (Dudley, 6C/81). John aka James and Lydia had 9 known children in Stoke-on-Trent; William (b. ~1860), Hannah (b. ~1864), Harriet (b. ~1866, died in infancy), Elizabeth aka Lizzie (b. ~1867), Thomas (b. ~1870), Sarah Ann (b. ~1871), Mary Ann (b. ~1873), Lydia Ellen (b. 4 Q. 1879) and Harriet (b. ~1883). Daughter Lydia Ellen Steventon was born in 4th Quarter 1879 (Stoke-on-Trent, 6B/251).

In 1891, James Steventon, 55, a forge labourer in an iron works, at 67 Hicken's Row, Stoke-on-Trent, with wife Lydia, 49, children Elizabeth, 24, Sarah Ann, 21, both breeze washers, Lydia, 12, at home, and Harriet, 8, a scholar. John Steventon, 55, died in 1st Quarter 1893 (Dudley, 6C/19). In 1901, Lydia Steventon, 61, a widow, at 4 New Cross Street, Tipton, Stoke-on-Trent, with her married daughter Mary Ann Timmins, 28, and her family. Lydia Steventon nee Whitehouse, 70, died in 1914 (Dudley, 6B/1011).

Ray's maternal great-grandparents –
Thomas Mason and Ann Newcombe

Ray's maternal great-grandfather Thomas Mason was born around 1833 in Oldcoates, Nottinghamshire and his great-grandmother Ann Newcombe (or Newcomb) was born around 1836 in Torworth, Nottinghamshire. Thomas Mason, an agricultural labourer, married Ann Newcombe in 2nd Quarter 1856 (Sheffield, 9C/422). Thomas and Ann had 5 known sons; in Sheffield, George F (b. ~1857), William H (b. ~1859); in Oldcoates, John S (b. ~1869), Charles Newcombe (b. ~1873) and in Langwith, Herbert (b. 27 September 1874).

In 1871, Thomas Mason, 37, an agricultural labourer, resided in Oldcoates, with wife Ann, 35, sons George F, 14, an under-gardener, William H, 12, a farm boy, and John S, 2. In 1881, Thomas Mason, 47, a horse keeper at a colliery, resided in Bolsover, Derbyshire, with wife Ann, 45, sons George, 24, a stone mason, John, 12, Charles, 8, Herbert, 6, and a niece Gertrude Newmill, 9, all scholars. In 1891, Thomas Mason, 58, an ostler groom, at 46 Newgate Lane, Mansfield, with wife Ann, 55, sons Charles, 18, an apprentice, and Herbert, 16, an apprentice.

By 1901, Thomas Mason, 67, living on his own means, at 135 Newgate Lane, Mansfield, with wife Ann, 65. Thomas Mason, 69, died in 1903 (Mansfield, 7B/66) and wife Ann Mason nee Newcombe, 72, died in 1908 (Mansfield, 7B/54).

Ray's maternal great-grandparents –
Frederick Berridge and Elizabeth Davenport

Ray's other maternal great-grandfather Frederick Berridge was born illegitimately around 1835 in Mansfield, Nottinghamshire to his mother Sarah Berridge (b. ~1811, Mansfield). In 1851, Frederick, 16, a brick turner, resided in Littleworth, Mansfield, with his unmarried mother Sarah Berridge, 40, a factory hand. Frederick and his first partner Emma Wilkinson had 2 known daughters; Sarah A (b. ~1858, Sheffield) and Lucy (b. ~1862, Attercliffe). In 1861, Frederick Berridge, 25, a wood turner, at 16 Hollands Square, Sheffield, Yorkshire, with Emma, 22, daughter Sarah A, 3, brother-in-law Matlock Wilkinson, 26, a cordwainer, and wife Louisa Wilkinson, 23, a boot binder. Emma Wilkinson died in 1865 in Sheffield.

Ray's great-grandmother Elizabeth Davenport (or Devonport) was born around 1834 in Mansfield. Elizabeth Davenport, who was married previously to Thomas Espley in 3rd Quarter 1860 in Mansfield, had daughters Eliza A. Devonport (b. ~1857, illegitimate), Emma Espley (b. ~1862) and son Thomas Espley (b. ~1865).

In 1871, Frederick Berridge, 36, a widowed wood turner, resided in Banniers Court, Mansfield, with daughters Sarah A, 13, Lucy, 9, both factory hands, Elizabeth Espley, 37, a housekeeper, with her children Eliza A Devonport, 14, a factory hand, Emma Espley, 9, and Thomas A Espley, 6, both scholars. Although both Frederick and Elizabeth recorded they were married, neither of their spouses were present and it is likely they cohabited as husband and wife.

The following year, Frederick Berridge married second wife Elizabeth Espley in 1st Quarter 1872 (Nottingham, 7B/280). Daughter Alice Berridge was born in 1st Quarter 1874 (Mansfield, 7B/88). Frederick and Elizabeth also had another daughter Elizabeth A (b. ~1881, Mansfield).

In 1881, Frederick Berridge, 45, a wood turner, at 1 Bowmar Court, Mansfield, with wife Elizabeth, 46, daughters Alice, 7, a scholar, Elizabeth A, 4 months old, stepdaughter Emma Espley, 19, a factory hand, stepson Thomas Espley, 16, a blacksmith, and grandson John Espley, 3 months old. In 1891, Frederick Berridge, 55, a wood turner, at 2 Nottingham Road, Mansfield, with wife Elizabeth, 56, daughters Alice, 17, a doubler at a cotton mill, and Elizabeth, 10, a scholar. Frederick Berridge, 61, died in 1896 in Mansfield and wife Elizabeth Berridge nee Davenport, 70, died there in 1905.

CHAPTER 4

Nobby Stiles MBE (right half)

Honours as an England player:
1 FIFA World Cup 1966
1 EUFA European Championship (Bronze medallist) 1968

D elivered in the cellar of the family home during a German Luftwaffe air raid, Norbert Peter Stiles MBE was born on 18 May 1942 at 263 Rochdale Road, Collyhurst, Manchester, to parents Charles Anthony Stiles, an undertaker's manager, and Catherine Byrne aka Kitty as registered in May 1942 (Manchester, 8D/452). On the same evening Manchester was blitzed, RAF bombers conducted retaliatory air raids on Mannheim in Germany. Stiles grew up in Collyhurst, a poor working-class district of North Manchester. He was raised in the Roman Catholic faith and attended the local St Patrick's Catholic Primary School. His father Charlie was the manager of an undertaker's parlour in the Stiles family business. His mother Kitty supplemented the family income by working as a factory machinist.

Stiles was an English professional footballer and manager, playing for England for five years, winning 28 caps and scoring one goal. He played every minute of England's victorious 1966 World Cup campaign. In the tournament semi-final against Portugal, he was given the job of marking the prolific Portuguese forward Eusébio. His tough performance resulted in Eusébio being practically nullified for the entire game. Stiles also played in the victorious final, England winning 4–2 against West Germany.

Stiles, on winning his 20th cap, had no man-marking brief in the final against West Germany. Instead he played a strong, tough match as England saw a 2–1 lead levelled with the last kick of the game, before Geoff Hurst completed a hat-trick to win the competition in extra time. At the final whistle, Stiles did a spontaneous jig with the Jules Rimet Trophy in his hand, while holding his false teeth in the other. His iconic dance has gone down in World Cup folklore.

Stiles played in the next four internationals. He was judged to have performed poorly as World Champions England famously lost 3–2 to Scotland at Wembley in 1967 and he was dropped by Ramsey. As an aside, the author's father Archie, a locomotive driver in Glasgow, travelled to the game with railway mates on a football special from Glasgow to Wembley, to watch the Scots' victory over the Auld Enemy. The author remembers watching the game on the family's small black and white Phillips television.

Stiles was selected in the England squad for the 1968 European Championships, however, the holding role in midfield was handed to Tottenham Hotspur's Alan Mullery. Stiles was recalled for the third-place play-off game against the Soviet Union. Ramsey selected him for the 1970 World Cup finals in Mexico. He did not play in any matches, with England knocked out in the quarter finals. After the tournament, his England career ended.

Stiles spent the majority of his club career for Manchester United, spending eleven years at Old Trafford. He became renowned for his tough tackling and ball-winning qualities. With the Red Devils, he won two League titles and the 1968 European Cup under legendary Sir Matt Busby. Stiles is one of only three Englishmen, alongside Bobby Charlton, Manchester United, and Ian Callaghan, Liverpool, to have won both World Cup and European Cup medals. Stiles also had short spells with Middlesbrough (1971–73) and Preston North End (1973–75).

Nobby's parents –
Charles Anthony Stiles and Catherine Byrne

Nobby's father Charles Anthony Stiles aka Charlie was born on 22 April 1916, during WWI, to parents Herbert Stiles and Elizabeth Alice Taylor (Manchester, 8D/442). His mother Catherine Byrne aka Kitty was born on 17 October 1914, during WWI, to parents Joseph Byrne and Catherine Giblin (Manchester, 8D/472). In 1921, Charles

DEREK NIVEN

Anthony Stiles, 5, at school, lived with father Herbert Stiles, an undertaker, and mother Elizabeth Alice at 263 Rochdale Road, Collyhurst, Manchester, along with his siblings. Charles was raised in the Roman Catholic faith. After leaving school he got a job in the family undertaking business, following in the footsteps of his father and grandfather.

Charles Anthony Stiles, 21, an undertaker, married Catherine Byrne, 22, a machinist, in 3rd Quarter 1937 (North Manchester, 8D/1032). By the time WWII broke out the Stiles family was still living in the poor working class district of Collyhurst, North Manchester. In 1939 War Register, Charles A Stiles, born 22 April 1916, a motor driver, still at 263 Rochdale Road, Manchester, with wife Catherine, born 17 October 1914, doing unpaid domestic duties, and son Charles A Stiles, born 24 May 1938, under school age.

Son Norbert Peter Stiles was born on 18 May 1942 during an air raid in Collyhurst, Manchester, to parents Charles Stiles and Catherine Byrne aka Kitty. At that time, Charlie worked as the manager of an undertaker's parlour for Stiles Funeral Services on Rochdale Road. His wife Kitty supplemented the family income by working as a factory machinist. Charles and Kitty celebrated their son Nobby's success on 30 July 1966 at Wembley.

Catherine Stiles nee Byrne, 69, died in March 1984 (Manchester, 38/757). Charles Anthony Stiles, 74, a retired undertaker's manager, died in 1990 in Manchester. The funeral business continued trading in Collyhurst as Stiles &

Kennedy Funeral Services until converted to M K Kennedy Funeral Services in 2012, still based in Collyhurst.

Nobby's paternal grandparents –
Herbert Stiles and Elizabeth Alice Taylor

Nobby's paternal grandfather Herbert Stiles was born on 24 February 1888 in Manchester to parents Charles Stiles, an undertaker, and Catherine Burke. In 1891, Herbert, 1, at 249 Rochdale Road, Collyhurst, Manchester, with father Charles Stiles, 35, an undertaker, mother Catherine, 31, and his two brothers. In 1901, Herbert, 11, still resided there with father Charles Stiles, 44, a funeral furnisher, mother Catherine, 42, and his siblings.

Nobby's paternal grandmother Elizabeth Alice Taylor was born on 8 January 1888 in Lancashire to parents Robert Taylor, a cotton spinner, and Nancy Aspden (Oldham, 8E/488). In 1891, Elizabeth A, 3, at 11 Canterbury Street, Oldham, with father Robert Taylor, 27, a cotton spinner, mother Nancy, 27, and his sister Mary A, 1. In 1901, Elizabeth, 13, a cotton winder, at 1 Canterbury Street, Oldham, with father Robert Taylor, 37, a cotton mill winder, mother Nancy, 37, a cotton winder, siblings Mary A, 11, and John A, 8.

Herbert Stiles married Elizabeth Alice Taylor in 2nd Quarter 1908 in Prestwich, Greater Manchester (Bury, 8D/511). Herbert and Elizabeth Alice had 4 known children in Manchester; Herbert (b. 20 December 1908), Elizabeth

Alice (b. 2 Q. 1910), Charles Anthony (b. 22 April 1916) and Clifford Gerrard (b. 30 April 1921).

In 1911, Herbert Stiles, 24, a hydraulic packer in a shipping warehouse, at 11 Ashford Street, Beswick, Manchester, with wife Elizabeth Alice, 24, son Herbert, 2, and daughter Elizabeth Alice, 11 months old. Son Charles Anthony Stiles was born on 22 April 1916, during WWI, in Manchester to parents Herbert Stiles and Elizabeth Alice Taylor (Manchester, 8D/442).

Herbert later joined his father Charles' funeral business, Stiles Funeral Services in Rochdale Road. In 1939 War Register, Herbert Stiles, born 24 February 1888, a funeral director and employer, at 111 Rochdale Road, Collyhurst, Manchester, with wife Elizabeth Alice, born 8 January 1888, doing unpaid domestic duties, and son Clifford, born 30 April 1921, a motor mechanic. In 1941, son Clifford Gerrard Stiles, service number 1508085, enlisted in the Royal Air Force. Elizabeth Alice Stiles nee Taylor, only 57, died in 1945 and husband Herbert Stiles, 71, died in 1961, both in Manchester.

Nobby's paternal grandparents – Robert Taylor and Nancy Aspden

Nobby's other paternal grandfather Robert Taylor was born around 1864 in Royton, Oldham, Lancashire. Nobby's maternal grandmother Nancy Aspden was born on 14 June

1863 in Blackburn, Lancashire to parents James Aspden (b. ~1826, Blackburn) and Elizabeth (b. ~1822, Bradford, Yorkshire). In 1881, Nancy, 17, a speed tenter in a cotton mill, at 25 Shaw Road, Royton, Oldham, with father James Aspden, 55, mother Elizabeth, 58, and his sister Mary Ann, 28, a cotton winder, born around 1853 in Blackburn. A 'tenter' was an old occupational name describing a machine attendant. Nancy's job was to ensure the constant speed of the cotton reels.

Robert Taylor married Nancy Aspden in 2nd Quarter 1887 (Oldham, 8D/838). Daughter Elizabeth Alice Taylor was born on 8 January 1888 to parents Robert Taylor, a cotton spinner, and Nancy Aspden (Oldham, 8E/488). They also had another daughter Mary Ann (b. ~1890) and a son John A. (b. ~1893), both born in Oldham.

In 1891, Robert Taylor, 27, a cotton spinner, at 11 Canterbury Street, Oldham, with wife Nancy, 27, daughters Elizabeth A, 3, and Mary A, 1. He lived at the home of his mother-in-law Elizabeth Aspden, 69, and sister-in-law Mary, 38, a cotton winder, (b. ~1853, Blackburn). In 1901, Robert Taylor, 37, a cotton mill winder, at 1 Canterbury Street, Oldham, with wife Nancy, 37, a cotton winder, children Elizabeth, 13, a cotton winder, Mary A, 11, and John A, 8. Nancy Taylor nee Aspden, only 40, died in 1903 (Oldham, 8D/428).

Nobby's maternal grandparents –
James Byrne and Mary Ann Giblin

Nobby's maternal grandfather James Byrne was born on 13 April 1876 in Dublin, Ireland. James Byrne married first wife Mancunian-born Margaret Flynn in 1898 in Manchester and they had 2 known sons there; James Henry (b. ~1900) and Daniel (b. ~1901). In 1901, James Byrne, 25, a gas works labourer, at 19 Windsor Street, Collyhurst, Manchester, with wife Margaret, 25, and son James Henry, 1. Margaret Byrne nee Flynn, only 29 years-old, died in early 1905 in Prestwich, Bury, Greater Manchester.

Nobby's grandmother Mary Ann Giblin was born on 8 April 1881 in Manchester to parents Joseph Giblin, a general labourer, and Irish-born Catherine Scott. In 1891, Mary A, 10, at 36 Stonehewer Street, St Michael, Manchester, with her widowed father Joseph Giblin, 42, a labourer in a floor cloth works, brothers Joseph, 16, a warper in a cotton mill, and William, 14, a railway porter. In 1901, Mary A, 19, still resided there with her widowed father Joseph Byrne, 52, a general labourer.

James Byrne married second wife Mary Ann Giblin in 4th Quarter 1905 (Prestwich, 8D/680). They had 8 known children in Manchester; Margaret (b. ~1907), Joseph (b. 2 November 1909), Christopher (b. 23 December 1910), Mary (b. 27 May 1913), Catherine (b. 4 Q. 1914), Thomas P (b. 4 Q. 1916), Elizabeth (b. 6 January 1919) and Peter W (b. 3 Q. 1921). In 1911, James Byrne, 33, an oil gas maker for the Lancashire & Yorkshire Railway Company, at 12 Franklin Street, Rochdale Road, Collyhurst, Manchester, with wife Mary Ann, 28, children James Henry, 11, Daniel, 10, Margaret, 4, Joseph, 1, and Christopher, 3 months old.

At the time, the L&YR Company was one of the largest railway groups in the country with Manchester Victoria being one of the largest stations in Britain. During the 1923 amalgamation of the railway companies, the L&YR became part of the huge London Midland & Scottish Railway Company. James Byrne was transferred to the LMS.

In 1939 War Register, James Byrne, born 13 April 1876, an LMS railway company oil gas maker, at 161 Waterloo Street, North Manchester, with wife Mary Ann, born 8 April 1881, doing unpaid domestic duties, children Joseph, born 2 November 1909, a sewerage labourer, Christopher, born 23 December 1910, a Corporation general labourer, Mary, born 27 May 1913, a shop assistant, and Elizabeth Smith nee Byrne, born 6 January 1919, a machinist. Mary Ann Byrne, 78, died in 1960 in Manchester and husband James Byrne predeceased her.

Nobby's paternal great-grandparents – Charles Joseph Stiles and Catherine Burke

Nobby's paternal great-grandfather Charles Joseph Stiles was born on 21 October 1855 in Liverpool, Lancashire to parents Charles Stiles (b. ~1825, Ireland) and Catherine Matthews (b. ~1826, Ireland) (Liverpool, 8B/31). The Stiles family lived in Hornby Street when Charles Joseph Stiles was baptized in St Francis Xavier Roman Catholic Church,

Salisbury Street, Everton, Liverpool on 11 November 1855. The priest was Fr C H Collyns and the sponsors were Richard Dickenson and Agnes Turner.

In 1903, Liverpool Corporation cleared 534 homes in Hornby Street, describing the street as:

> *'The insanitary houses were of the back-to-back type, situated in narrow and ill-ventilated courts, each court containing from ten to twelve houses. The sanitary arrangements were very defective, in many cases one convenience being used by the occupants of five or six houses.'*

In 1861, Charles J Stiles, 5, at 288 Great Howard Street, Liverpool with his mother Catherine Stiles, 35, a widowed furniture broker. In 1871, Charles, 12, a scholar, boarded at the home of the Irish-born O'Neill family at 5a Moor Street, Manchester, with widowed mother Catherine Stiles, 50, now working as a dressmaker. Although Charles was nearer 16, Catherine may have lied about his age to keep him in school and ensure he received a proper education, ultimately beneficial to his future.

Nobby's paternal great-grandmother Catherine Burke was born around 1859 in Manchester, Lancashire to Irish-born parents John Burke (b. ~1823) and Ann (b. ~1828). It is likely John and Ann Burke, with son Martin, emigrated from Ireland to Liverpool around 1852, later moving to Manchester. This was to escape the ravages of the devastating Irish Potato Famine (1846–52). Over 1 million Irish perished through starvation, disease and destitution and over another million emigrated to Britain, Australia and the USA.

John's brother Peter Burke immigrated to Liverpool around 1840 and in 1841, Peter Burke, 15, resided in an overcrowded tenement in Adlington Street, Liverpool. In 1851, Peter Burke, 26, an unmarried agricultural labourer, was recorded as a prisoner in the House of Correction and County Gaol in Kirkdale, Walton-on-the-Hill, West Derby. Peter was recorded as born in County Galway around 1825, suggesting Galway is the birthplace of the Burke family. Peter was subjected to hard labour and the gaol's treadmill used for grinding corn was the largest in England. It needed the efforts of 130 prisoners a day to work it.

Kirkdale House of Correction in North Dingle Lane had one of the highest death rates in the country for a prison. A report written at the time produced the following information about its prisoners: 50% unable to name months of the year, 39% unable to name the reigning monarch, 43% ignorant of the words 'virtue', 'vice' and 'righteousness' and 15% unable to count to 100.

Private 1924 John Burke, born around 1823 in Milltown, County Galway, enlisted in the 40th Regiment of Foot on 10 July 1841 in Liverpool. John, 18, a clerk, was described as an Irish Catholic, height 5 feet 4½ inches, fair complexion, grey eyes and fair hair.

Charles Stiles married Catherine Burke in 1st Quarter 1881 (Manchester, 8D/304). In 1881, Charles Stiles, 24, a poultry dealer, at 16 Heelis Street, Manchester, with wife Catherine, 21, a dressmaker, at the home of father-in-law John Burke,

57, a hawker, mother-in-law Ann, 53, and Catherine's older brother Martin Burke, 30, (b. ~1851, Ireland). Also living there was Catherine's Uncle Peter Burke, 55, a hawker, with an Irish-born boarder Richard Mulroy, 38, a street scavenger, and his son John Mulroy, 18, an iron works labourer.

Charles and Catherine had 8 known children in Manchester; John (b. ~1882), Bernard (b. ~1887), Herbert (b. 24 February 1889), Clifford (b. ~1892), Gertrude (b. ~1895), Violet (b. ~1896), Philomena (b. ~1898) and Norbert (b. ~1900). Son Herbert Stiles was born on 24 February 1888 in Manchester, Lancashire to parents Charles Stiles, an undertaker, and Catherine Burke.

In 1891, Charles Stiles, 35, an undertaker, at 249 Rochdale Road, Collyhurst, Manchester, with wife Catherine, 31, sons John, 9, a scholar, Bernard, 3, and Herbert, 1. Also staying with Charles was his wife's unmarried Irish-born Uncle Peter Burke, 62, a hawker. In 1901, Charles Stiles, 44, a funeral furnisher and employer, still resided there with wife Catherine, 42, sons John, 19, a funeral conductor, Bernard, 14, a schoolboy, Herbert, 11, Clifford, 9, Norbert, 9 months old, daughters Gertrude, 6, Violet, 5, and Philomena, 3. Also at Charles's home were Ellen Smith, 22, a general domestic servant, and the ubiquitous Uncle Peter Burke, 70, a general porter.

Charles and Catherine's son Norbert Stiles, a leather maker by trade, who Nobby Stiles was named after, enlisted during WWI. The family lived at 42 Greenheys Lane, Manchester. Private 3916 Norbert Stiles, 7th Lancashire Fusiliers, enlisted at Salford on 10 July 1915. However, he was discharged two days later on 12 July 1915, after being found to be under enlistment age. Norbert had been caught up in patriotic fervour, however, by 1915, the army made more thorough checks to ensure young boys were not sent to the slaughterhouse in France and Flanders.

Greenheys Lane is a short walk east of Old Trafford, where Nobby Stiles later made his name at Manchester United. It is unknown if son Herbert served, however, son Bernard enlisted as a Driver with the Army Service Corps, arriving in France on 15 May 1915 and awarded the 1915 Star, the British War and Victory medals.

Charles Stiles, 64, an undertaker, died in 1926 in Manchester South. In 1939 War Register, Catherine Stiles, born 27 August 1859, a widow doing household duties, still resided alone at 42 Greenheys Lane, Manchester. Catherine Stiles nee Burke, 79, died in 1941 in Stockport, Lancashire.

Nobby's maternal great-grandparents –
Joseph Giblin and Catherine Scott

Nobby's maternal great-grandfather Joseph Giblin was born around 1849 in Salford, Greater Manchester to parents James Giblin, a cotton weaver, (b. ~1823, Billericay, Essex) and Mary Ann (b. ~1824, Manchester). Nobby's great-grandmother Catherine Scott was born around 1840 in Castlebar, County Mayo, Ireland to parents Thomas Scott, a shoemaker, (b. ~1806, Castlebar) and Harriet (b.~1808, Castlebar). The Scotts emigrated to Little Bolton,

Manchester following the Irish Potato Famine around 1852, living there throughout the 1860s. Catherine worked in a cotton mill.

Joseph Giblin married Catherine Scott in 3rd Quarter 1872 (Manchester, 8D/767). In 1881, Joseph Giblin, 32, a labourer, at 36 Stonehewer Street, Manchester, with wife Catherine, 36, a hose maker, sons Joseph, 5, a scholar, and William, 3. Also lodging there were Andrew Hines, 36, a labourer, his Irish-born mother Mary S Hines, 60, a greengrocer, Thomas Sweeney, 36, a poulterer, Catherine Cunningham, 26, a fish hawker, and their daughter Ann Sweeney, 3.

Catherine Giblin nee Scott, 44, died in 1891 (Manchester, 8D/244). In 1891, recently widowed Joseph Giblin, 42, a floor cloth works labourer, still at 36 Stonehewer Street, Manchester, with children Joseph, 16, a warper in a cotton mill, William, 14, a railway porter, and Mary A, 10. By 1891, the earlier floor oil cloths were usually produced by Joseph's employer, Thomas Witter & Company, as the newer linoleums, which were aggressively marketed and more widely available to the working classes. In 1901, Joseph Giblin, 52, a widowed general labourer, still resided there with his daughter Mary A, 19. Joseph Giblin, 75, died in 1924 in Manchester.

CHAPTER 5

Jack Charlton OBE DL (Centre half)

Honours as an England player:

1 FIFA World Cup 1966

1 EUFA European Championship (Bronze medallist) 1968

4 British Home Championships

J ohn Charlton OBE DL aka Jack was born on 8 May 1935 in the coal mining village of Ashington, Northumberland, near Morpeth, to parents Robert Charlton, aka Bob, and Elizabeth Ellen Milburn, aka Cissie. Known in the family as 'Wor Kid', Jack was the elder brother of Bobby Charlton of Manchester United and England. Refer to Chapter 8. Born into a footballing family in Ashington, Charlton was initially overshadowed by his younger brother Bobby, who was signed by Manchester United. Meanwhile Jack was on national service with the Household Cavalry. His footballing uncles were Jack Milburn (Leeds United and Bradford City), George Milburn (Leeds United and Chesterfield), Jim Milburn (Leeds United and Bradford Park Avenue) and Stan Milburn (Chesterfield, Leicester City and Rochdale). The legendary Newcastle United and England footballer Jackie Milburn was his mother Cissie's cousin.

Ashington's economy was based entirely on coal mining. Although his family had a strong footballing pedigree, his father made a living as a coal miner. Jack was the eldest of four brothers – Bobby, Gordon and Tommy – and the frugal finances of the family meant all four brothers shared the same bed. His father Bob had no interest in football. However, his mother Cissie played football with her children and later coached the local school team. As teenagers, Cissie took her sons to watch Ashington and Newcastle United play, and Charlton remained a lifelong Newcastle supporter. Nowadays, professional footballers earn millions. However, back then, Cissie had learned by watching her Milburn brothers, getting her sons into professional football was the route out of grinding poverty in Ashington.

Aged 15, Charlton was offered a trial at Leeds United, where his Uncle Jim played at left-back, although he turned it down to work with his father in mining. He worked in the mines for a short time, handing in his notice after finding out how difficult and unpleasant it was to work deep underground. He applied to join the police force, while reconsidering the offer from Leeds United. His Leeds trial clashed with his police interview, and Charlton chose to play in the game. The trial was a success and he joined the ground staff at Elland Road.

Charlton was a professional English footballer and manager who played in defence. He played at centre-half for the England team that won the 1966 World Cup. He later managed the Republic of Ireland national team from 1986 to 1996 achieving two World Cup and one European Championship appearance. He spent his entire club career with Leeds United from 1950 to 1973, helping the club to the Second Division title (1963–64), First Division title (1968–69), FA Cup (1972), League Cup (1968), Charity Shield (1969), Inter-Cities Fairs Cup (1968 and 1971), as well as promotion from the Second Division (1955–56) and five second-place finishes in the First Division, two FA Cup final defeats and one Inter-Cities Fairs Cup final defeat. His 629 league and 762 total competitive appearances are club records. In 2006, Leeds United supporters voted Charlton into the club's greatest XI.

Called up to the England team days before his 30th birthday, Charlton scored six goals in 35 international games and appeared in two World Cups and one European Championship. He played in the World Cup final victory over West Germany in 1966. He helped England finish third in Euro 1968 and win four British Home Championship tournaments. He was named FWA Footballer of the Year in 1967.

After retiring from playing he became a manager, and led Middlesbrough to the Second Division title in 1973–74, winning the Manager of the Year award in his first season as a manager. His first signing was Bobby Murdoch, Celtic's 1967 European Cup winner. Charlton kept Middlesbrough as a stable top-flight club until his resignation in April 1977. He took charge of Sheffield Wednesday in October 1977 and led the club to promotion out of the Third Division in 1979–80. He left the Owls in May 1983, and served Middlesbrough as caretaker-manager at the end of the 1983–84 season. He managed Newcastle United in 1984–85. He took charge of the Republic of Ireland national team in February 1986, leading them to their first World Cup in 1990, where they reached the quarter-finals. He also led the nation to Euro 1988 and the 1994 World Cup. He resigned in January 1996 and retired from football.

Jack's parents –
Robert Charlton and Elizabeth Ellen Milburn

Jack's father Robert Charlton aka Bob was born on 24 May 1909 in Ashington, Northumberland to parents Robert Charlton and Margaret Laidler (Morpeth, 10B/463). Jack's mother Elizabeth Ellen Milburn aka Cissie was born on 11 November 1912 to parents John Thomas Milburn and Elizabeth Ann Charlton in Ashington (Morpeth, 10B/911). Robert Charlton, a coal miner, married Elizabeth Ellen Milburn in 3rd Quarter 1934 (Morpeth, 10B/1015). In 1939 War Register, Robert Charlton, born 24 May 1909, a coal cutter doing heavy work in a coal mine, at 46 Hawthorn

Road, Ashington, with wife Ellen, born 11 November 1912, doing unpaid domestic duties, and two sons, marked as 'record officially closed'.

Robert and Cissie had 4 known sons in Ashington; John aka Jack, Robert aka Bobby, Gordon and Thomas aka Tommy. Cissie was from the famous Milburn family of professional footballers. She encouraged her sons to play professionally, planning their route out of the grinding poverty of the Ashington mining economy. Her sons Jack and Bobby both made it to the pinnacle of world football. They won medals galore in English football, in Europe and with England at Wembley in the 1966 World Cup.

Bob had to apologise to his sons for being unable to attend the semi-final game against Portugal, where son Bobby scored the winner, as he was booked for a shift at the Ashington pit. However, Robert and Cissie celebrated Jack and Bobby's double medal haul on 30 July 1966. Robert Charlton, 72, a retired coal miner, died in 1982. Elizabeth Ellen Charlton nee Milburn, 84, died in 1996.

Jack's paternal grandparents –
Robert Charlton and Margaret Laidler

Jack's paternal grandfather Robert Charlton was born in 3rd Quarter 1888 in Humshaugh, Northumberland to parents Robert Charlton, a mason, and Agnes Jessie Grant (Hexham, 10B/319). In 1891, Robert, 2, resided in Walwick, Hexham with father Robert Charlton, 48, a mason, mother Agnes J,

29, and his siblings. Robert's father Robert Charlton died in 1897 and his mother Agnes took the family north to her birthplace in Scotland. In 1901, Robert, 14, an apprentice grocer, at 11 Middle Street, Prestonpans, East Lothian, with his mother Agnes J Charlton, 41, a widow, and his siblings.

Jack's paternal grandmother Margaret Laidler was born in 3rd Quarter 1888 to parents William Laidler and Mary Kelly (Glendale, 10B/412). Robert met Margaret in spring 1908 and she fell pregnant with their son Robert. Robert Charlton, a coal miner, married Margaret Laidler in 3rd Quarter 1908 (Tynemouth, Northumberland, 10B/443). Son Robert Charlton aka Bob was born on 24 May 1909 in Ashington to parents Robert Charlton and Margaret Laidler (Morpeth, 10B/463). Robert Charlton, 66, died in 1953 and his wife Margaret Charlton nee Laidler, 64, also died in 1953.

Jack's maternal grandparents –
John Thomas Milburn and Elizabeth Ann Charlton

Jack's maternal grandfather John Thomas Milburn was born in 2nd Quarter 1886 to parents John Tanner Milburn and Elizabeth Brown (Morpeth, 10B/375). His grandmother Elizabeth Ann Charlton was born in 4th Quarter 1889 in Newcastle-upon-Tyne to parents George Charlton and Esther Fisher. John Thomas Milburn, a coal miner, married Elizabeth Ann Charlton in 4th Quarter 1907 in Ashington (Morpeth, 10B/683).

John and Elizabeth had 6 known children in Ashington; John aka Jack (b. ~1908), George William (b. ~1910), Elizabeth Ellen aka Cissie (b. 1912), James aka Jim (b. ~1919), Gladys (b. ~1922) and Stanley aka Stan (b. ~1926). Their 4 sons all played professional football; Jack (Leeds United and Bradford City), George (Leeds United and Chesterfield), Jim (Leeds United and Bradford Park Avenue) and Stan (Chesterfield, Leicester City and Rochdale). John and Elizabeth's nephew was the renowned Jackie Milburn (Newcastle United and England).

John Edward Thompson Milburn, known as 'Wor Jackie' in the Geordie dialect, was born on 11 May 1924 at 14 Sixth Row, Ashington, to parents Alexander Milburn, a coal miner, and Annie Thompson. His cousin Cissie Charlton nee Milburn was the mother of Jack and Bobby Charlton. He is the second highest goal scorer for Newcastle United, only surpassed by Alan Shearer. He won the FA Cup three times with Newcastle and the Irish Cup with Linfield. Milburn also received 13 caps with England and is an inductee into the English Football Hall of Fame.

Elizabeth Ann Milburn nee Charlton, only 53, died in 1942, during WWII (Northumberland Central, 10B/455) and husband John Thomas Milburn, 63, died in 1949 (Northumberland Central, 1B/339).

Jack's paternal great-grandparents –
Robert Charlton and Agnes Jessie Grant

Jack's paternal great-grandfather Robert Charlton was born around 1843 in Warden, Hexham, Northumberland. His great-grandmother Agnes Jessie Grant aka Janet or Jessie was born on 7 April 1860 in Dalkeith, Midlothian, Scotland to Irish father John Grant and Scottish mother Janet Bullock aka Jessie. Janet was the daughter of David Bullock, an Edinburgh printer of Candlemaker Row, born around 1786. David died in 1849 at Anchor Close, High Street.

John Grant, a hawker (b. ~1818, Ireland) was almost certainly Protestant, born in Ulster. John Grant, a shoemaker, married Janet Bullock (b. ~1821, Cowgate, Edinburgh) on 19 February 1839 in Canongate Church, Edinburgh. The Old Parish Register for Canongate (Ref. 685/3/166) is as follows:-

Grant & Bullock: 15th February 1839: John Grant, shoemaker, Dickson's Lodgings, Plainstone Close, Canongate, Cottage Church Parish, and Janet Bullock, Burkhart's Lodgings, No.247 Canongate, New Street Parish, and in the original parish of Canongate, daughter of David Bullock, printer, Candlemaker Row, Edinburgh, gave up their names for proclamation of marriage, certified by Andrew Sandilands, printer, Candlemaker Row, and the above named David Bullock and Mr David Arthur, one of the Elders of New Street Parish. The above named parties were three times regularly proclaimed,

in the parish churches of Canongate and New Street,
on Sabbath, the 17th, and no objections being offered,
they were married on 19th current, by the Rev James
Scott, Relief Minister, Edinburgh.

Plainstanes Close was off 222 Canongate on the Royal Mile and is now the Canon's Gait pub. In the 16th century Mary Queen of Scots' French tailor Jacques de Soulis lived at Plainstanes Close, nicknamed Bloody Mary's Close. Nearby 247 Canongate is now an aparthotel. Candlemaker Row was named after the still extant Candlemaker's Hall (Nos. 36–42) built in 1722 by the Incorporation of Candlemakers. It was once the main thoroughfare out of Edinburgh from the Grassmarket near Edinburgh Castle.

John and Jessie had 4 known children; David (b. ~1843, Edinburgh), Thomas (b. ~1856, Dalkeith), James (b. ~1858, Dalkeith) and Agnes Jessie aka Janet (b. 7 April 1860, Dalkeith). In 1861, baby Janet, 1, resided in West Dalkeith with father John Grant, 43, a hawker, mother Jessie, 38, and her siblings. By 1871, her father John Grant was dead and Agnes, 10, a scholar, at Gordon's Close, High Street, Dalkeith, with her widowed mother Jessie, 50, a hawker, Thomas, 17, a scholar, and James, 13, an apprentice iron moulder. Also visiting Jessie was her brother, Thomas Bullock, 48, a hammerman from Cowgate, Edinburgh.

In the 1852–53 Ordnance Survey Name Book, Gordon's Close is described as 'a close branching off the High Street West. And opening again upon the same it is bounded by dwelling houses on both sides. Chiefly in good repair and occupied by Tradesmen, it is the property of Mr Gordon, hence the name.'

Robert Charlton had 2 known children from a first marriage born in Humshaugh; Thomas E (b. ~1872) and Mary E (b. ~1877). Robert Charlton married his second wife Agnes Jessie Grant on 14 May 1881 in Humshaugh (Hexham, 10B/419). Robert and Agnes had 12 known children; in Humshaugh, James (b. ~1882), William Stoker (b. ~1883), Elizabeth Thompson (b. ~1884), George (b. ~1885), David (b. ~1886), Robert (b. ~1887); in Warden, Temple (b. ~1889), Alexander (b. ~1890), Agnes Jessie (b. ~1891), Sarah Jane (b. ~1893), Isaac (b. ~1895) and Annie (b. ~1897).

In 1891, Robert Charlton, 48, a mason, resided in Walwick, Hexham, with wife Agnes J, 29, children Thomas E, 19, a cartman, Mary E, 14, James, 9, William S, 8, Elizabeth T, 7, George, 6, David, 5, Robert, 2, Temple, 1, and Alick, 6 months old. Robert Charlton, 54, died in 1897 in Hexham. After husband Robert's death, Agnes took her children north to Scotland.

In 1901, Agnes J Charlton, 41, a widow, at 11 Middle Street, Prestonpans, East Lothian, with children James, 19, William, 18, George, 16, David, 15, all coal miner hewers or drawers, Robert, 14, an apprentice grocer, Temple, 12, Alexander, 11, Agnes Jane, 10, Sarah, 9, Isaac, 6, all scholars, and Annie, 4. In the 1939 Electoral Register for Newcastle-upon-Tyne, Agnes J Charlton was a registered voter at 11 Duke Street. In 1939 War Register, Agnes J Charlton, born 7 April 1860, doing unpaid domestic duties, at 26 Shieldfield Green, Newcastle-upon-Tyne. Agnes Jessie

Charlton nee Grant, 81, died the following year in 1940, during WWII, in Newcastle, Northumberland.

Jack's paternal great-grandparents –
William Laidler and Mary Ann Kelly

Jack's other paternal great-grandfather William Laidler was born around 1862 and his great-grandmother Mary Ann Kelly was born around 1865. William Laidler married Mary Ann Kelly in 2nd Quarter 1884 (Alnwick, 10B/553) and they had a known daughter Margaret (b. 3 Q. 1888, Glendale). Mary Ann Laidler nee Kelly, 31, died in 1897 in South Shields, Northumberland and her husband William Laidler, 65, died in 1927 in Alnwick.

Jack's maternal great-grandparents –
John Tanner Milburn and Elizabeth Brown

Jack's maternal great-grandfather John Tanner Milburn was born around 1863 and his great-grandmother Elizabeth Brown was born around 1865. John Tanner Milburn married Elizabeth Brown in October 1883 (Morpeth, 10B/556). John and Elizabeth had 12 known children; Robert (b. ~1884), Thomas William (b. ~1885), John Thomas (b. 2 Q. 1886), Sarah Jane (b. ~1889), Elizabeth Ellen (b. ~1891),

Florence (b. ~1893), Margaret (b. ~1894), James (b. ~1896), William (b. ~1898), Alexander (b. ~1902), Samuel (b. ~1904) and Phyllis Baird (b. ~1907). John Tanner Milburn, 59, died in 1922 in Morpeth and his wife Elizabeth Milburn nee Brown, 77, died in 1942, during WWII, in Northumberland Central.

Jack's maternal great-grandparents – George Charlton and Esther Fisher

Jack's other maternal great-grandfather George Charlton was born around 1862 and his great-grandmother Esther Fisher was born around 1863. Given the Charlton surname, it is possible George Charlton on the maternal line was somehow related to Jack and Bobby Charlton on the paternal line. George Charlton married Esther Fisher in 1883 (Gateshead, 10A/1228) and they had a daughter Elizabeth Ann (b. 4 Q. 1889) in Newcastle-upon-Tyne.

CHAPTER 6

Bobby Moore OBE (left half)

Honours as an England player:

1 FIFA World Cup 1966

1 UEFA European Championship (Bronze medallist) 1968

4 British Home Championships

Robert Frederick Chelsea Moore OBE aka Bobby was born on 12 April 1941 in Upney Hospital, Barking, Essex, to parents Robert Edward Moore aka Big Bob and Doris Smaggasgale Joyce Buckle aka Doss. As an only child, he was a shy boy, almost introverted, and did not seek the limelight. At school he was nicknamed 'Tubby' Moore, as he carried youthful puppy fat, which he grew out of, although the nickname stuck for some years. Moore was a perfectionist, learned from his mother Doss, who even washed and ironed his bootlaces before every game. He always stood out as a smart, stylish dresser.

Commentators noted Moore was the antithesis of the younger George Best. Moore represented the tidy, freshly-scrubbed post-war children of the Spitfire generation, while Best depicted the modern, scruffy, rebellious spirit of the Beatlemania era.

Moore attended Westbury Primary School in Barking, then Tom Hood Secondary School in Leytonstone, playing football at both. He was an English professional footballer, who most notably played for West Ham United, captaining the club for more than ten years. In 1956, Moore joined West Ham and, after advancing through their youth set-up, played his first game on 8 September 1958 against Manchester United. He was also captain of the England team that won the 1966 World Cup. He is highly respected as one of the greatest defenders in football history, and Pelé cited Moore as the greatest defender he ever faced.

Widely regarded as West Ham's greatest player, Moore played over 600 games for the Hammers during a 16-year tenure. He won the FA Cup in 1963–64 and the UEFA Cup Winners' Cup in 1964–65. During his club career, he won the FWA Footballer of the Year in 1964 and the West Ham Player of the Year in 1961, 1963, 1968 and 1970. In August 2008, West Ham United officially retired the number 6 shirt in honour of Moore.

Moore was made England's captain in 1964, aged 23, lifting the World Cup trophy in 1966. He won 108 caps for his country, which at the time of his international retirement in 1973 was a national record. An England national team icon, a bronze statue of Moore stands at the entrance to Wembley Stadium, inscribed:

> 'Immaculate footballer. Imperial defender. Immortal hero of 1966. First Englishman to raise the World Cup aloft. Favourite son of London's East End. Finest legend of West Ham United. National Treasure. Master of Wembley. Lord of the game. Captain extraordinary. Gentleman of all time.'

A composed central defender, Moore was best known for his reading of the game and ability to anticipate opposition movements. This distanced him from the image of the hard-tackling, high-jumping defender. Receiving BBC Sports Personality of the Year in 1966, he was the first footballer to win the award. The following January, Moore was given an OBE in the New Year's Honours List. Moore had a cameo role in the 1981 film *Escape to Victory*. The film is about a team of British POWs planning an escape following a match against their German counterparts. Starring Sylvester Stallone, Max von Sydow and Michael Caine, there were also cameo roles for footballers Pelé, Ozzie Ardiles, Werner Roth, Mike Summerbee and John Wark, among others. Bobby Moore was inducted into the English Football Hall of Fame in 2002 in recognition of his impact on the English game.

Bobby's parents –
Robert Edward Moore and Doris Smaggasgale Joyce Buckle

Bobby's father Robert Edward Moore aka 'Big Bob' was born on 24 April 1913 in London to parents Robert James Moore and Rose Hetty Sipthorpe (Poplar, 1C/1045). When Bob was just 2-years-old, his father Private Robert Moore was killed in WWI at the Battle of the Aisne on 15 September 1915. His mother Rose remarried his stepfather James Cooper in 1916 in Poplar.

In 1921, Robert, 8, still lived in Poplar with his mother Rose and stepfather James Cooper. After leaving school Big Bob became a railway signalman. In 1939 War Register, Robert E Moore, born 24 April 1913, a railway signalman, at 17 Carmen Street, Poplar, with his mother Rose Cooper, born 3 September 1886, doing unpaid domestic duties, step-father James Cooper, born 29 July 1877, a Thames lighterman and Air Raid Precautions Post Warden, and his siblings.

Bobby's mother Doris Smaggasgale Joyce Buckle aka Doss was born on 11 November 1912 in Barking, Essex to parents Frederick Buckle, a soap manufacturer's labourer, and Beatrice Elizabeth Louisa Smaggasgale (Romford, 4A/1160). Doris was born a twin with her sister, Dora Gladys Joan Buckle. In 1939 War Register, Doris J Buckle (later pencilled in Moore), a dressmaker's presser, born 11 November 1912, at 110 Faircross Avenue, Barking, Essex, with father Frederick Buckle, born 14 February 1880, a soap manufacturer's warehouse checker, mother Beatrice E L, born 4 July 1876, doing unpaid domestic duties, and sisters.

As war drums beat again, Robert Moore married Doris Buckle in September 1939 in Essex (Ilford, 4A/2011). Big

Bob worked as a maintenance man lagging the pipes and scaling the boilers at the coal-fired Barking Power Station, coming home each day covered in coal dust. Son Robert Frederick Chelsea Moore was born on 12 April 1941 in Upney Hospital, Barking (Ilford, 4A/409).

A few days later, on 16 April 1941, the family home at 43 Waverley Gardens was badly shaken by German Luftwaffe bombing. *The Times* reported it as 'one of the most wanton and savagely indiscriminate raids of the war', with a thousand Londoners killed that evening. The mayor of Barking's car was commandeered to transport those in emergencies. Around midnight, the car took Bob and Doss, carrying baby Bobby, across Barking to her parents Fred and Beatrice Buckle's home at 110 Faircross Avenue. Doss's sister Georgina, aka Aunt Ina, grabbed hold of young Bobby and they all hunkered down for the night to ride out the Blitz. The Germans targeted Barking Power Station but it survived the war unscathed, as did the family home at 43 Waverley Gardens. However, it took six weeks of clearing debris before Bob and Doss could return home with Bobby.

In 1971, as they appeared alongside their son Bobby on the TV show '*This is Your Life*', Doss scolded husband Bob for giving away the secret that she, previously a dressmaker's presser, used to wash and iron young Bobby's football kit – including his bootlaces. Robert Moore, 65, died in June 1978 (Newham, Essex, 4A/1242). Doris Joyce Moore nee Buckle, 79, died in 1992 (Havering, Essex, 13/278).

Bobby's paternal grandparents –
Robert James Moore and Rose Hetty Sipthorpe

Bobby's paternal grandfather Robert James Moore was born in 4th Quarter 1884 in Cubitt Town, London to parents George Robert Moore aka Robert and Eliza Howell (Millwall, 1C/716). In 1891, Robert J, 6, a scholar, at 30 Manchester Road, Poplar, with father Robert Moore, 27, a stationary engine driver in the London docks, mother Eliza, 28, and brother Charles W, 3. In 1901, Robert J, 16, a cooper, still resided there with father Robert Moore, 35, a stationary engine driver, mother Eliza, 36, brother Charles W, 13, a scholar, and Uncle Albert Moore, 27, (b. ~1873, Gissing, Norfolk).

On 25 October 1901, Robert Moore, 18, enlisted in Norwich as Private 5932 1st Battalion Royal Norfolk Regiment. He was described as a box maker by trade, 5 feet 9 inches tall, with a fresh complexion, hazel eyes and light brown hair. He was based at home until 1 October 1903, serving detention for 'drunkenness on duty' on 2 October 1902. Then followed a tour of duty in India from 2 October 1903 until 26 December 1904, sailing then for peacekeeping duties in South Africa, where he was based from 27 December 1904 until 16 February 1907. He served with the Norfolks until 21 October 1909, then transferred to army reserve. Robert intended to work as a box maker and live at 37 Russell Street, Paul Road, Bow. Anticipating war, Robert re-engaged for a further 4 years from 22 October 1913.

Bobby's paternal grandmother Rose Hetty Sipthorpe aka Rosetta was born on 3 September 1886 in Limehouse,

London to parents Thomas Henry Sipthorpe, a labourer, and Sarah Amelia Arnold. Rosetta Sipthorpe was baptized by Rev W Forster on 21 January 1887 at St Paul's Church, Bow Common, Tower Hamlets. The family lived at 33 Endive Street, Limehouse. In 1888, the family were still at 33 Endive Street and Rose's father Thomas Sipthorpe was a registered elector.

In 1901, Rose H, 14, a worker in Bryant & May's match factory, at 41 Harford Street, Mile End, Poplar, with father Thomas Sipthorpe, 52, a builder's labourer, mother Sarah, 53, a laundress on her own account working from home, and her 2 brothers. Bryant & May's Fairfield Works in Bow employed about 2,000 workers, mostly young girls. At only 14, Rose could expect to earn no more than 4 or 5 shillings a week. This was a very risky job, especially for girls working with dangerous white phosphorus. They ran the risk of catching the dreaded 'phossy jaw'.

In 1911, Rose Hetty, 25, a laundress and ironer, at 49 St Dunstan's Road, Mile End, London, with her widowed mother Sarah Amelia Sipthorpe, 64, a laundress on her own account working from home, and brother Thomas James, 23, a packing case maker.

Robert Moore, 27, a railway goods porter, of 73 Arcadia Street, Poplar, married Rose Hetty Sipthorpe, 26, of 54 Arcadia Street, Poplar, on 15 December 1912 at St Saviour's Church (Poplar, 1C/1057). The wedding was conducted by Rev Vincent Smith, minister; the best man was Thomas James Wild and the best maid was Louisa Margaret Carpenter. Rose was heavily pregnant at the time. Son Robert Edward

Moore was born on 24 April 1913 in London to parents Robert Moore and Rose H Sipthorpe (Poplar, 1C/1045).

Son George Alexander Moore was born in 3rd Quarter 1914 (Poplar, 1C/1027). Shortly before son George's birth, Robert Moore re-enlisted on 1 August 1914 at Stratford, London as Private 5932 1st Battalion Royal Norfolk Regiment. When war broke out the battalion was billeted in Holywood, Belfast. The battalion sailed to Le Havre, France in mid-August as part of the British Expeditionary Force.

Robert remained in reserve while the battalion fought at the Battle of Mons on 23 August 1914. He was involved in the subsequent retreat to protect Paris from the German Army. Along with the French Fifth Army and the BEF, Robert remained in reserve as the Norfolks fought at the Battle of Le Cateau on 26 August 1914. The following day, Robert's company was called into front line action on 27 August 1914 as the Norfolks advanced to attack at the important 1st Battle of the Marne from 5 to 12 September 1914, when the Entente forces successfully halted the German advance and saved Paris from capture.

As the Germans retreated back to the River Aisne, the Norfolks were thrown straight into the Battle of the Aisne from 12 to 15 September. The British and French Allied forces faced Von Kluck's German First Army and Von Bŭlow's Second Army. Private Robert Moore was killed in action on 15 September 1914. Robert's body was never recovered. He is commemorated at the La Ferte-Sous-Jouarre Memorial to the Missing in the Seine-et-Marne region near Paris. He was awarded the 1914 Star with Mons clasp, the British War and Victory Medals, eventually presented to his widow Rose. At the time of his death Rose lived at 15 Ellesmere Street, Poplar, later moving to 17 Carmen Street, Poplar.

Rose Hetty Moore, 30, a widow, remarried James George Cooper, 36, a Thames lighterman, both of 29 Woolmore Street, Poplar, on 23 April 1916 in All Saints Church, Poplar. The witnesses were Thomas James Wild and Amelia Elizabeth Peterken. On 7 July 1919, Rose Hetty Cooper received a War Gratuity pension of £2 12s 7d for herself and her children. In respect of Robert's medals, Rose had written the following letter to the War Office:-

> *Mrs Cooper, 17 Carmen St, Poplar E14, Late Mrs Moore: Just a line to you regards of my late Husband's medals as he was called up on the 1ˢᵗ August 1914 and he was killed the 15ᵗʰ of September 1914 and I have only Received the Mons Star and bar. Sir I am given to understand that all medal and Ribbons have been issued but I have not received any. Sir I think I have waited long enough for my Late Husband's Medals which I am Intitled (sic), Private Robert Moore, 1ˢᵗ Norfolk Regiment.*

Rose had written again to the army and the medals issue was not finally resolved until 1922.

In 1921, Rose Hetty Cooper still resided in Poplar with husband James, son Robert and 4 others. In 1939 War Register, Rose Cooper, born 3 September 1886, doing unpaid domestic duties, at 17 Carmen Street, Poplar, with husband James Cooper, born 29 July 1877, a Thames lighterman and Air Raid Precautions Post Warden, son Robert E Moore, born 24 April 1913, a railway signalman, and 3 other children with 'records officially closed'.

Rose Hetty Cooper nee Sipthorpe (previously Moore), 66, died in 1953 (Romford, 5A/767).

Bobby's maternal grandparents – Frederick Buckle and Beatrice Elizabeth Louisa Smaggasgale

Bobby's maternal grandfather Frederick Buckle aka Fred was born on 14 February 1880 in Bromley, Middlesex to parents William Buckle and Elizabeth Ann Doughty. On 27 June 1887, Frederick Buckle, age 7, was enrolled in Bow High Street School by his father William Buckle, of 4 Three Mill Lane, West Ham. In 1911, Frederick, 21, a soap dresser, at 40 Bruce Road, Poplar, Bromley, with father William Buckle, 55, a shoemaker on his own account, mother Elizabeth A, 60, and his 2 siblings. Fred grew up to become a '17-stone giant of a man'.

With a name straight out of a Dickensian novel, Bobby's grandmother Beatrice Elizabeth Louisa Smaggasgale was born on 4 July 1876 in Acton, Middlesex to parents Edwin Smaggasgale and Caroline A Eakins (Brentford, 3A/104). In 1881, Beatrice, 4, at 11 Atley Street, Bow, London, with father Edwin Smaggasgale, 26, a railway engine driver, mother Caroline, 23, sister Maud, 2, and brother Edwin, 2 weeks old. On 26 May 1884, Beatrice Smaggasgale, age 7, was enrolled in Atley Road School, Tower Hamlets by her father Edwin Smaggasgale, of 70 Lefevre Road, Bow. Edwin Smaggasgale died in April 1888 in Poplar.

In 1891, Beatrice, 14, at 17 Christian Buildings, Devons Road, Bromley, with her widowed mother Caroline A Smaggasgale, 32, and her siblings. In 1901, Beatrice E L Smaggasgale, 24, a confectionery sweet and bread maker, at 59 Bruce Road, Poplar, Bromley, with her sister, Maud L, 22, a storewoman at a watch factory.

Frederick Buckle married Beatrice Elizabeth Louisa Smaggasgale on 21 June 1902 in All Saints Church, West Ham, Essex. Fred and Beatrice had 7 known children, 2 died in infancy before 1911; the others were Frederick George Edwin (b. 15 January 1906, Bromley), Georgina Maud Rosemary (b. 7 February 1910, Bromley), twins Dora Gladys Joan and Doris Smaggasgale Joyce (b. 11 November 1912, Barking) and Beatrice Ethel Lilian (b. 13 January 1919, Barking). On 14 February 1906, son Frederick George Edwin Buckle, of 4 Spey Street, Bromley, was baptized in St Leonard's Church, Bromley. Daughter Georgina Maud Rosemary Buckle (Bobby's Aunt Ina) was baptized, age 6, on 12 July 1916 in St Margaret's Church, Barking.

In 1911, Frederick Buckle, 31, a soap manufacturer's labourer, r at 4 Spey Street, Poplar, Bromley, with wife Beatrice, 33, children Frederick G E, 5, and Georgina M, 1. Given the gap in children between 1912 and 1919, Frederick Buckle enlisted in WWI, possibly Sergeant Frederick Buckle in the 6th City of London Rifles Territorial Force.

By the end of WWI, the Buckle family had moved to 110 Faircross Avenue, Barking. They were still there in 1921, where Fred still worked in the soap works. This was almost certainly the Royal Primrose Soap Works in nearby Knights Road, Silvertown, situated in the docklands between Poplar and Barking. The soap works factory was opened by John Knight when Fred was born in 1880. It is now part of the multinational Unilever Group.

In 1939 War Register, Frederick Buckle, born 14 February 1880, a soap manufacturer's warehouse checker, still at 110 Faircross Avenue, Barking, with wife Beatrice E L, born 4 July 1876, doing unpaid domestic duties, twin daughters Dora G (later Englefield), a tobacconist's saleswoman, and Doris J (later Moore), a dressmaker's presser, both born 11 November 1912, and Beatrice E L (later Hardwick), a shipping clerk, born 13 January 1919. On the night of 16 April 1941, Fred and Beatrice's home became the shelter from a severe German bombing raid on Barking, including son-in-law Robert Moore, daughter Doris and four-day-old grandson Bobby Moore.

Frederick Buckle, 68, died on 22 February 1948 in Ilford, Essex. His wife Beatrice E L Buckle nee Smaggasgale, 88, died in September 1965 in Worcester, Worcestershire.

Bobby's paternal great-grandparents – George Robert Moore and Eliza Howell

Bobby's paternal great-grandfather George Robert Moore aka Robert was born in 4th Quarter 1865 in Poplar, London to parents Robert Moore, a stationary engine driver, and

Mary Crisp, although he spent most of his childhood in Norfolk. Bobby's great-great-grandparents Robert Moore and Mary Crisp were born around 1840 in Tibenham, Depwade, Norfolk to local farming folk. They were married on 31 October 1860 in Tibenham Church by F Watson, curate.

In 1871, Robert, 5, a scholar, born in London, at Long Row, Gissing, Norfolk, with father Robert Moore, 30, a farmer of 12 acres, mother Mary, 30, a farmer's wife, siblings William, 10, Frederick, 7, both scholars, Walter J, 2, and Charles, 1. In 1881, Robert, 15, an agricultural labourer, at 1 Broad Way End, Gissing, with father Robert Moore, 41, an engine proprietor, mother Mary, 41, siblings William, 20, an engine driver, Frederick, 17, Walter J, 12, both agricultural labourers, Charles, 11, Alfred, 9, Albert, 8, Eliza, 7, Mary Ann, 5, all scholars, Fanny, 3, and Elizabeth, 1.

Bobby's great-grandmother Eliza Howell was born in 1st Quarter 1862 in Battersea, London to parents James Howell (b. ~1821, Chesham, Bucks) and Ann Maria Welham (b. ~1823, Bergholt, Suffolk) (Wandsworth, 1D/444). Eliza was baptized on 14 February 1863 in St Mary Newington, Southwark to parents James Howell, a labourer, and Ann Maria, of Petherton Street, Southwark. In 1881, Eliza, 20, a domestic servant, at 15 Marshfield, Poplar, with father James Howell, 60, a labourer at Millwall Docks, mother Anne M, 58, and brothers James, 30, and Thomas, 22, both labourers at Millwall Docks.

G. Robert Moore, 21, a labourer, who signed with his 'x' mark, married Eliza Howell, 21, both of Poplar, London,

in Poplar Church on 19 July 1884. The wedding was con-
ducted by T W Nowell, minister; the best man was Charles
James Mills and the best maid was Christina Noakes. In
1891, Robert Moore, 27, a stationary engine driver in the
London docks, at 30 Manchester Road, Poplar, with wife
Eliza, 28, sons Robert J, 6, a scholar, and Charles W, 3.
In 1901, Robert Moore, 35, a stationary engine driver, still
resided there with wife Eliza, 36, sons Robert J, 16, a cooper,
Charles W, 13, a scholar, and his younger brother Albert
Moore, 27, a stationary engine driver (b. ~1874, Norfolk).
George Robert Moore, 40, died in 1904 (Poplar, 1C/329).
Eliza Moore nee Howell, 50, died in 1913, in Mile End,
London.

Bobby's paternal great-grandparents - Thomas Henry Sipthorpe and Sarah Amelia Arnold

Bobby's other paternal great-grandfather Thomas Henry
Sipthorpe (or Sibthorpe and variants) was born around
1850 in Enfield, Middlesex to parents Thomas and Sarah
Sipthorpe. In 1851, Thomas, 7 months old, lived in
Parsonage Lane, Enfield. In 1861, Thomas, 10, a scholar, at
Anderson's Yard, off Baker Street, Enfield, with his parents
Thomas Sipthorpe, 31, a labourer, and Sarah, 30.

In 1871, Thomas Sipthorpe, 20, a barman, at the home
of Watson Ansell, 34, a licensed victualler. This was at the
Magpie & Stump, 18 Old Bailey, London, across the street
from Newgate Prison, now the Old Bailey Courthouse. Up

until 1868, just three years before Thomas joined the Magpie & Stump, the publican let out upstairs rooms to London bigwigs to watch the popular public hangings at Newgate, giving it the nickname of the 'Horror Hanging Pub'. The landlord would send a 'last pint' of Two-Penny, a type of pale ale, across to the cell of the condemned man before he met his fate.

In 1837, Richard Harris Barham penned:

> *"The clock strikes Twelve – it is dark midnight – Yet the Magpie and Stump is one blaze of light, ale glasses and jugs, and rummers and mugs, cold fowl and cigars, pickled onions in jars, And there is Sir Carnaby Jenks, of the Blues, All come to see a man die in his shoes."*

The last man to be publicly hanged in front of the Old Bailey was Michael Barrett in 1868, for his part in the Clerkenwell Explosion by the Irish Republican Brotherhood, killing 12 people. The pub was also mentioned in Charles Dickens' novel *The Pickwick Papers*.

Bobby's great-grandmother Sarah Amelia Arnold was born in 3rd Quarter 1849 in Westminster, London to parents Charles Arnold, a painter/plumber, and Isabella Ann Till, of 29 West Street (now St Barnabas Street), Belgravia, and baptized on 12 August 1849, along with brother George Frederick (b. ~1847), in St Paul's Church, Wilton Place, Knightsbridge. In 1851, Sarah, 1, at 44 Queen Street (now Pimlico Road), Belgravia, with father Charles Arnold, 45, (b. ~1806, Finchley), mother Isabella, 36, (b. ~1815, Pimlico), and her siblings.

No marriage record has been found for Thomas and Sarah. In 1881, Thomas Sipthorpe, 31, a bricklayer's labourer, at 14 Endive Street, Limehouse, with reputed wife Sarah, 31, and son Richard, 1. On 5 March 1883, Thomas Sipthorpe was sentenced to 3 months imprisonment at Clerkenwell Court of General Session for larceny and receiving.

In a case of history repeating itself, Bobby Moore had been again selected by Alf Ramsey as captain of England for the 1970 Mexico World Cup. Moore was implicated in the theft of a bracelet from a jeweller in Bogotá, Colombia, where England were involved in a warm-up game. A young assistant claimed Moore removed the bracelet from the hotel shop without paying for it. Moore had been in the shop with Bobby Charlton, although no proof was offered to support the accusations. Moore was arrested and released. On the return flight to Mexico, the team plane from Ecuador stopped back in Colombia. Moore was detained and placed under four days house arrest. Diplomatic pressure, plus weak evidence, eventually saw Moore exonerated.

Thomas and Sarah had 5 known children; in Limehouse, Richard (b. ~1880), Marian (b. ~1883), Rose Hetty aka Rosetta (b. 1886), Thomas James (b. ~1888) and Stepney, George (b. ~1892). Daughter Rose Hetty Sipthorpe aka Rosetta was born on 3 September 1886 in Limehouse, London. Rosetta Sipthorpe was baptized by Rev W Forster on 21 January 1887 at St Paul's Church, Bow Common, Tower Hamlets. The family lived at 33 Endive Street, Limehouse. In 1888, the family were still at 33 Endive

Street and Thomas Sipthorpe was a registered elector for Limehouse district.

In 1901, Thomas Sipthorpe, 52, a builder's labourer, at 41 Harford Street, Mile End, London, with wife Sarah, 53, a laundress on her own account working from home, children Rose H, 14, a worker in Bryant & May's match factory, Thomas, 13, and George, 9. Thomas Sipthorpe, 49, died on 10 March 1902 of tubercular phthisis (tuberculosis) as certified by Dr J Harley Brooks, medical superintendent in the Mile End Old Town Infirmary. Thomas was buried in Bow Cemetery by undertakers Faulkner.

Bobby's maternal great-grandparents – William Buckle and Elizabeth Ann Doughty

Bobby's maternal great-grandfather William Buckle was born around 1846 in Steventon, Berkshire and his great-grandmother Elizabeth Ann Doughty was born around 1840 in Mitford, Norfolk. William and Elizabeth had 3 known children in Bromley; Frederick aka Fred (b. 14 February 1880), Ethel (b. ~1884) and Ernest J (b. ~1887). Son Frederick Buckle aka Fred was born on 14 February 1880 in Bromley, Middlesex to parents William Buckle and Elizabeth Ann Doughty. On 27 June 1887, William Buckle, of 4 Three Mill Lane, West Ham, enrolled his son Frederick Buckle, age 7, in Bow High Street School.

In 1901, William Buckle, 55, a shoemaker on his own account, at 40 Bruce Road, Poplar, Bromley, with wife Elizabeth A, 60, children Frederick, 21, a soap dresser, Ethel, 17, a tailoress working at home, and Ernest J, 13. The following year, William Buckle, only 56, died in 1902 (Poplar, 1C/367). Elizabeth Ann Buckle nee Doughty, 80, died in 1922 (Poplar, 1C/304).

Bobby's maternal great-grandparents – Edwin Smaggasgale and Caroline A Eakins

Bobby's other maternal great-grandfather Edwin Smaggasgale was born around 1855 in Shoreditch, London to parents William Smaggasgale, a tin plate maker, (b. ~1816, Shoreditch) and Hannah Payne (b. ~1819, Shoreditch). In 1861, Edwin, 8, at 27 Herbert Street, Shoreditch, with father William, 45, a tin plate maker, mother Hannah, 42, siblings Louise, 19, Alfred, 15, William, 13, and Emily, 4. Also living there was Edwin's grandfather John Smaggasgale, 76, a widowed tin plate worker (b. ~1784, Shoreditch). John's deceased wife was Mary Ann Rollings.

Bobby's great-grandmother Caroline A Eakins was born around 1858 in Bow, London, to father William Eakins, a railway driver, making her a true Cockney. Edwin Smaggasgale, a railway fireman, married Caroline Eakins on 5 April 1875 in St John's Church, Limehouse Fields (Stepney, 1C/820). Neither Edwin nor Caroline could read or write, signing the marriage register with their 'x' marks.

There is no known derivation for the Smaggasgale surname, however, due to the element of illiteracy, it may actually be an Anglicized corruption of the Scottish surname MacAskill, from the Gaelic 'Mac Asgaill', meaning 'son of the cauldron of the gods'. Clan MacAskill were renowned for being tall and warlike. Records show the Smaggasgale surname was predominant in London. It is likely Bobby's great-great-great-grandfather John Smaggasgale was the progenitor of the corrupted surname. It would certainly be appropriate to call Bobby Moore a 'son of the cauldron of the gods' for his 1966 Wembley triumph.

Edwin and Caroline had 5 known children in Bromley; Beatrice Elizabeth Louisa (b. 4 July 1876), Maud Lillian (b. ~1878), Edwin George W (b. 1881, d. 1 Q. 1882), George (b. ~1883) and Edwin (b. ~1887). Daughter Beatrice Elizabeth Louisa Smaggasgale was born on 4 July 1876 in Acton, Middlesex (Brentford, 3A/104).

In 1881, Edwin Smaggasgale, 26, a railway engine driver, at 11 Atley Street, Bow, London, with wife Caroline, 23, children Beatrice, 4, Maud, 2, and Edwin, 2 weeks old. Son Edwin George W Smaggasgale, under a year old, died in 1882 in Poplar. In 1884, Edwin and his family lived at 70 Lefevre Road, Bow and his daughter Beatrice attended Atley Road School, Tower Hamlets. Edwin Smaggasgale, 38, died in April 1888 (Poplar, 1C/344). He was buried on 21 April 1888 in Newham Cemetery, London.

In 1891, Caroline A Smaggasgale, 32, a widow, at 17 Christian Buildings, Devons Road, Bromley, with children Beatrice, 14, Maud, 12, an apprentice milliner, George, 8, a scholar, and Edwin, 4. Out of economic necessity with four young children, Caroline Smaggasgale married second husband William Page in 1ˢᵗ Quarter 1894 in Poplar. Caroline A Page nee Eakins (previously Smaggasgale), 57, died in 1916 (Romford, 4A/517).

CHAPTER 7

Alan Ball MBE (outside right)

Honours as an England player:
1 FIFA World Cup 1966

Four days after VE Day, Alan James Ball MBE was born on 12 May 1945 at his grandparents' home at 2 Brookhouse Avenue, Farnworth, Lancashire to parents James Alan Ball, aka Alan Sr., a serving soldier, and Violet Duckworth. Ball was an English professional football player and manager. At 21, he was the youngest member of England's 1966 World Cup winning team. He played in midfield for numerous clubs, including Blackpool, Everton, Arsenal and Southampton. He scored over 180 league goals in a career spanning 22 years. Ball started his football career as a schoolboy, playing for Ashton United, the team his father managed. He played in the hurly-burly of the Lancashire Combination League.

Ball attended St Peter's Church of England School and Farnworth Grammar School. He fell out with his headmaster over missing games for the school team due to playing for Wolverhampton Wanderers. After leaving Farnworth Grammar with no qualifications, Wolves decided against signing Ball. The midfielder then started training with Bolton Wanderers, although they too decided not to sign him, as manager Bill Ridding thought he was too small.

Blackpool signed him after his father Alan Sr. called in a favour with the coach. Ball was trialled in September 1961 and was signed as an apprentice. He turned professional in May 1962, debuting on 18 August 1962 against Liverpool at Anfield in a 2–1 victory. Aged 17 years and 98 days, he became Blackpool's youngest league debutant. On 21 November 1964, Ball scored his first hat-trick, in a 3–3 draw with Fulham at Craven Cottage. His playing career also included a record £220,000 transfer from Everton to Arsenal at the end of 1971.

In the 1966 World Cup final, the 98,000 crowd at Wembley witnessed Ball's magnificent personal performance. Full of running, he continued to work, sprint and track back while teammates and opponents alike were exhausted. In extra time, the image of him running around the Wembley pitch with socks around his ankles is a lasting memory of the historic victory. Ball returned to a civic reception in Walkden, Lancashire, following World Cup success, where he lived with his parents and sister.

After retiring as a player, he had a 15-year managerial career, including spells in the top flight of English football with Portsmouth, Southampton and Manchester City.

Alan's parents –
James Alan Ball and Violet Duckworth

Alan Ball's father James Alan Ball aka Alan Sr. was born on 26 September 1924 in Farnworth, Bolton, Lancashire to parents James Ball and Elizabeth McGowan (Bolton, 8C/444). His mother Violet Duckworth aka Val was born in 3rd Quarter 1924 in Farnworth to parents Norman Duckworth and Eva Fitton (Bolton, 8C/469). James Alan Ball, 20, a soldier in His Majesty's Forces and professional footballer, of 2 Bentinck Street, Farnworth, married Violet Duckworth, 20, of 2 Brookhouse Avenue, Farnworth, on Christmas Day, 25 December 1944 in St Peter's Church, Farnworth (Bolton, 8C/778). The wedding was conducted by Rev J Lenehan; the best man was William Woods and the best maid was Lilian Ball, James's sister.

Son, Alan James Ball was born on 12 May 1945 in Farnworth to parents James Alan Ball, still serving with the army in Germany, and Violet Duckworth. Daughter Carolyn L Ball was born in 4th Quarter 1947 in Farnworth.

Like his son Alan, Ball was a professional English footballer and manager. Ball played as an inside forward for Bolton Boys Federation, Southport, Birmingham City, Oldham Athletic and Rochdale between 1945 and 1952. Ball started his managerial career in 1953 as player-manager of Oswestry Town. He then managed Borough United, Ashton United, where his son Alan had a spell as a player, and Nantwich. He managed the Cheshire side to a treble of Mid-Cheshire League, League Cup and Cheshire Amateur Cup in 1963–64.

In that famous summer of 1966, he left Nantwich to coach Stoke City. He then managed Halifax Town in two separate spells, 1967–1970 and 1976–1977, followed by Preston North End, 1970–1973, winning the Third Division title, then Southport, Swedish sides IF Saab and IK Sirius. Ball moved to central Stockholm and managed Djurgårdens IF in 1979.

Ball also worked as a publican at the Rose and Crown in Farnworth. While in Oswestry Town he was landlord of the King's Head in Church Street, Oswestry. He was tragically killed in a car accident in Nicosia, Cyprus in January 1982 aged 57. Ball was travelling to his next managerial position, with the Cypriot team Evagoras Paphos. He was being driven in a taxi from Larnaca Airport to start work when it crashed, killing him instantly.

At his death in 1982, Ball left his wife Violet a widow. He witnessed his son Alan Jr. win the 1966 World Cup and later saw Alan follow his father into football management. In April 2021, Ball's grandson, Jimmy, became the third generation of the family to manage in the Football League. He was appointed interim manager of Forest Green Rovers.

Alan's paternal grandparents –
James Ball and Elizabeth McGowan

Alan's paternal grandfather James Ball was born on 7 February 1904 in Rhos near Ruabon, Wrexham, Wales to parents James Ball, a coal miner, (b. ~1866, West Derby, Liverpool) and Miriam Hughes (b. ~1866, Rhos). Rhos is known in Welsh as Rhosllanerchrugog, 'the heathery glade'. The family moved from Wales to Farnworth around 1910. In 1911, James Ball, 7, at 7 Cole Street, Farnworth, with father James Ball, 45, an underground colliery hewer, mother Miriam, 45, and his siblings. His nationality was recorded as Welsh, owing to his birthplace.

Alan's grandmother Elizabeth McGowan was born on 23 October 1903 in Hindley, Lancashire to father Robert McGowan, a coal miner (Wigan, 8C/111). In 1911, Elizabeth, 7, at school, at 23 Victoria Street, Farnworth, with her widowed father Robert McGowan, 36, (b. ~1875, Liverpool) and her siblings.

James Ball married Elizabeth McGowan in 2nd Quarter 1924 (Bolton, 8C/711) and Elizabeth was pregnant with their son James. James and Elizabeth had 3 known children in Farnworth; James Alan (b. 26 September 1924), Lilian (b. 2 Q. 1926) and Trevor (b. 1 Q.1939). Son James Alan Ball was born on 26 September 1924 in Farnworth, Bolton to parents James Ball and Elizabeth McGowan.

In 1939 War Register, James Ball, born 7 February 1904, a joiner carpenter, at 2 Bentinck Street, Farnworth, with wife Elizabeth, born 23 October 1903, doing unpaid domestic duties, and one child marked as 'record officially closed', probably baby son Trevor. James Ball, 53, died in 1958 in Farnworth (Bolton, 10C/234) and wife Elizabeth Ball nee McGowan, 87, died in 1991 (Bolton, 38/8).

Alan's maternal grandparents – Norman Duckworth and Eva Fitton

Alan's maternal grandfather Norman Duckworth was born on 17 July 1902 in Farnworth, Bolton to parents James Duckworth and Elizabeth Alice Bulliss. In 1911, Norman, 8, at school, lodged at 22 Markland Square, Farnworth, with father James Duckworth, 55, a collier hewer, mother Elizabeth, 44, a cotton mill ring spinner, and younger brother Clifford, 3 months old. Alan's maternal grandmother Eva Fitton was born on 5 March 1905 in Bolton.

Norman Duckworth, 20, a colliery fireman, married heavily pregnant Eva Fitton, 17, in 1st Quarter 1923 (Bolton, 8C/644). Norman and Eva had 5 known children in Farnworth; Norman (b. 2 Q. 1923), Violet (b. 3 Q. 1924), James (b. 2 Q. 1927), Eileen (b. 2 Q. 1932) and Joyce E (b. 3 Q. 1933). Daughter Violet Duckworth was born in 3rd Quarter 1924 in Farnworth to parents Norman Duckworth and Eva Fitton (Bolton, 8C/469).

In 1939 War Register, Norman Duckworth, born 17 July 1902, a colliery fireman below ground, at 2 Barton Street, Farnworth, with wife Eva, born 5 March 1905, a cotton winder, and one child at home marked 'record officially closed'. Norman Duckworth, 77, died in 1979 (Bolton, 38/301) and wife Eva Duckworth nee Fitton, 87, died in 1992 (Salford, 39/760).

Alan's paternal great-grandparents – James Ball and Miriam Hughes

Alan's paternal great-grandfather James Ball was born in 4th Quarter 1865 in Lancashire (West Derby, 8B/391) and his great-grandmother Miriam Hughes was born in 1st Quarter 1866 in Rhos near Ruabon, Denbighshire, Wales to parents Robert and Ann Hughes (Wrexham, 11B/331). In 1871, Miriam, 5, at Poukey, Rhos, with father Robert Hughes, 42, (b. ~1829, Rhos), mother Ann, 28, (b. ~1843, Rhos) and her siblings. In 1881, Miriam Hughes, 15, a domestic servant, at 88 Huddersfield Road, Oldham. She lived at the home of George Marland, 29, a pattern maker, and his family.

James Ball married Miriam Hughes in Wrexham in 1888 and they had 13 known children, although 5 died in infancy; in Rhos, John (b. ~1888), Edith (b. ~1898), Robert (b. ~1899), Miriam (b. ~1902), and James (b. 7 February 1904); in Little Hulton, Doris (b. ~1908) and in Farnworth, Phyllis (b. ~1910).

In 1911, James Ball, 45, an underground collier hewer, at 7 Cole Street, Farnworth, with wife Miriam, 45, children Edith, 13, Robert, 12, both at school, Miriam, 9, James, 7, Doris, 3, and Phyllis, 1. Also staying there was son John Ball, 23, an underground collier hewer, with wife Sarah

Ann, 23, children Jessie Dora, 3, and Annie, 1. James Ball, 69, died in 1936 (Farnworth, 8C/526) and wife Miriam Ball nee Hughes, 72, died in 1938 (Farnworth, 8C/351).

Alan's maternal great-grandparents – James Duckworth and Elizabeth Alice Bulliss

Alan's maternal great-grandfather James Duckworth was born around 1856 in Little Lever, Lancashire. His great-grandmother Elizabeth Alice Bulliss was born in 1st Quarter 1869 in Little Lever to parents William and Jane Bulliss, both born around 1844 in Little Lever (Bolton, 8C/402).

James Duckworth, 44, married Elizabeth Alice Bulliss, 31, in 1st Quarter 1900 (Bolton, 8C/526). Marrying later in life, James and Elizabeth had 6 known children in Farnworth, however, 4 died in infancy. They included Norman (b. 1900, d. 1901), another Norman (b. 17 July 1902) and Clifford (b. March 1911).

In 1901, James Duckworth, 45, a coal miner hewer, at 67 Old Hall Street, Kearsley, Farnworth, with wife Elizabeth A, 32, and son Norman, 3 months old, who died later that year. Also residing there was his father-in-law William Bulliss, 54, a coal miner hewer, mother-in-law Jane, 53, and their other children. In 1911, James Duckworth, 55, a collier hewer, lodged at 22 Markland Square, Farnworth, with wife Elizabeth, 44, a cotton mill ring spinner, sons Norman, 8, at school, and Clifford, 3 months old.

Elizabeth Alice Duckworth nee Bulliss, 61, died in March 1931 (Bolton, 8C/432) and husband James Duckworth, 83, died in September 1939 (Farnworth, 8C/500).

CHAPTER 8

Sir Bobby Charlton CBE (inside right)

Honours as an England player:
1 FIFA World Cup 1966
1 EUFA European Championship (Bronze medallist) 1968
5 British Home Championships

Sir Robert Charlton CBE was born on 11 October 1937 in the coal mining village of Ashington, Northumberland, near Morpeth, to parents Robert Charlton aka Bob and Elizabeth Ellen Milburn aka Cissie. He was an English professional footballer who played in midfield and forward. Considered one of the greatest players of all time, he was a member of the England team that won the 1966 World Cup, the same year he won the Ballon d'Or. He played almost all of his club football at Manchester United. He was renowned for his attacking instincts, passing abilities from midfield and ferocious long-range shots, as well as his fitness and stamina. His older brother Jack, also in the World Cup-winning team, was a former defender for Leeds United and international manager for the Republic of Ireland. With success at club and international level, Bobby is one of the select players to win the World Cup, the European Cup and the Ballon d'Or.

His football career began with the East Northumberland Schools team. He was scouted to join Manchester United's 'Busby Babes' at age 15 in 1953. Aged 18, he debuted for the Manchester United first-team in 1956 and soon gained a regular place in the team. He became a Football League First Division champion in 1957, managed by the legendary Sir Matt Busby.

The following year in February 1958, Charlton played with United in a European Cup second leg tie against Red Star Belgrade in Yugoslavia. Charlton scored two goals, taking United into the semi-finals and the team flew back in a jubilant mood. The plane landed at Munich Airport to refuel in treacherous freezing conditions. After two aborted take-offs, some players and staff became nervous. Charlton and teammate Denis Viollet agreed to swap seats with Tommy Taylor and David Pegg, thinking they would be safer at the back. On the third take-off the plane skidded on slushy ice, clipped the boundary fence and a wing was sliced off hitting a house, causing the plane to crash.

Twenty three passengers died, including seven teammates killed at the scene, including Taylor and Pegg, with whom Charlton and Viollet had swapped seats prior to the fatal crash. Club captain Roger Byrne was killed, along with

Mark Jones, Billy Whelan, Eddie Colman and Geoff Bent. The legendary Duncan Edwards died a fortnight later from his severe injuries. Charlton survived the Munich air disaster after being rescued by his Northern Irish goalkeeping teammate Harry Gregg, heroically dragging Charlton and Viollet from the wreckage. Gregg also helped rescue Busby and Danny Blanchflower, both in a terrible way. Busby, a Catholic, was so badly injured he was given the last rites, but survived to rebuild United.

Five days before the disaster, the author's friend Robin Dale, doing his national service with the Royal Army Pay Corps at Hounslow, Middlesex, and a Manchester United fan, travelled across London to see the Red Devils play Arsenal at Highbury. In a frenetic and memorable game, United beat the Gunners 5–4, with goals from Taylor (2), Edwards, Charlton and Viollet. It was the last game the 'Busby Babes' played on English soil. On the 50th anniversary of Munich in 2008, the author and Robin travelled to Dudley, West Midlands to honour Duncan Edwards' grave.

After helping United win the FA Cup in 1963 and the Football League in 1965 and 1967, Charlton captained the Busby team that beat Benfica, led by Eusébio, to win the European Cup in 1968 at Wembley. He scored two goals in the final to help them become the first English club to win the competition. Charlton left Manchester United to become manager of Preston North End for the 1973–74 season, changing to player-manager the following season. He next accepted a post as a director at Wigan Athletic, then was appointed a member of Manchester United's board of directors in 1984.

At international level, Charlton was named in the England squad for four World Cups (1958, 1962, 1966 and 1970). At the time of his retirement from the England team in 1970 he had earned 106 caps. Charlton was the long-time record goal-scorer for Manchester United and England, and United's long-time record appearance maker – his total of 758 matches for United took until 2008 to be beaten, when Ryan Giggs did so in that year's Champions League final under Sir Alex Ferguson. With 249 goals, he was the club's highest all-time goal-scorer for more than 40 years, until Wayne Rooney surpassed it in 2017. Rooney had also claimed Charlton's England record, but in 2023 that has now been clinched by Harry Kane.

Bobby Charlton's ancestry

For Bobby Charlton's ancestry, refer to his brother, Jack Charlton, outlined in Chapter 5 above.

CHAPTER 9

Sir Geoff Hurst MBE (centre forward)

Honours as an England player:

1 FIFA World Cup 1966

1 EUFA European Championship (Bronze medallist) 1968

T he day after the Japanese attack on Pearl Harbor and the day President Franklin D Roosevelt addressed Congress with the 'Infamy Speech', Sir Geoffrey Charles Hurst MBE was born on 8 December 1941 in Ashton-under-Lyne, Tameside, Lancashire, to parents Charles Hurst, a serving soldier and professional footballer, and Evelyn M Hopkins. Hurst had two younger siblings; Diane and Robert. The family moved to Chelmsford, Essex when he was six years old, where he attended King's Road Primary School. His father, Charlie Hurst, was also a professional footballer who played for Bristol Rovers, Oldham Athletic and Rochdale. His mother, Evelyn Hopkins, was from a Gloucestershire family with a family legend that her mother's side was originally from Germany. Hurst is an English professional footballer. Under his father Charlie's management, Hurst played once for non-league Halstead Town Reserves when he was 'about 14'.

In the 1966 starting lineup Sir Alf Ramsey's preferred front two were Jimmy Greaves and Roger Hunt. Greaves and Hunt played in the three group games against Uruguay, Mexico and France. However, in the French game, Greaves suffered a deep gash to his leg, requiring stitches, and Hurst was chosen in the quarter-final against Argentina.

Argentina were a talented side, preferring a physically tough approach to the game, eventually reduced to ten men. The game was still tightly contested entering the final 15 minutes. However, Martin Peters swung over a curling cross from the left wing. Hurst, anticipating his Hammers club-mate's cross, got in front of his marker to glance a near post header past the Argentine keeper. England won 1–0 and reached the semi-finals.

Greaves was unfit for the Portugal game, so Hurst and Hunt continued up front. England won 2–1 thanks to two goals from Bobby Charlton, the second assisted by Hurst. As the final against the Germans approached, the media learnt of Greavsie's return to fitness and, while appreciating Hurst's contribution, called for the return of England's most prolific centre forward. Ramsey, however, remained resolute and selected Hurst for the final. Jimmy Greaves could not forgive Ramsey for leaving him out of the biggest game in English football history. However, Hurst paid the manager back in spades.

He famously became the first man to score a hat-trick in a World Cup final when England won 4–2 against West Germany at Wembley Stadium in 1966. Hurst's final burst forward happened as excited spectators spilled onto the edge of the field. This led to Kenneth Wolstenholme's legendary commentary of, *"they think it's all over…"*, followed by Hurst blasting the ball into the net with the last kick of the game and, *"…it is now!"*

Hurst began his career at West Ham United, where he scored 242 goals in 500 first-team appearances. At the Hammers he won the FA Cup in 1964 and the European Cup Winners' Cup in 1965. He was sold to Stoke City in 1972 for £80,000. After three seasons with Stoke, where he won the Watney Cup in 1973, he finished his Football League career with West Bromwich Albion in 1976. Hurst played football in Ireland at Cork Celtic and Seattle Sounders in the USA. He returned to England to manage non-league Telford United. He also coached in the England set-up before a two-year stint as Chelsea manager from 1979 to 1981. He later coached Kuwait SC before leaving the game to concentrate on his business commitments.

In total, Hurst scored 24 goals in 49 England appearances. As well as success at the 1966 World Cup he also appeared at the European Championships in 1968 and the 1970 World Cup. He also had a brief cricket career, appearing once for Essex in 1962, before concentrating on football.

Geoff's parents –
Charles Hurst and Evelyn M Hopkins

Geoff's father Charles Hurst aka Charlie was born on 25 January 1919 in Denton, Tameside, Lancashire, to parents James Edwin Hurst and Fanny Burt (Ashton-under-Lyne, 8D/513). His mother Evelyn M Hopkins was born in 1st Quarter 1918 in Gloucestershire to parents Francis William Hopkins and Louise Elizabeth Burton Blick (Dursley, 6A/373). Charles Hurst, a professional footballer currently engaged in war service, married Evelyn M Hopkins in 1st Quarter 1940 in Gloucestershire (Stroud, 6C/1441). They had three known children; Geoffrey Charles, Diane and Robert. Son Geoffrey Charles Hurst was born on 8 December 1941 in Ashton-under-Lyne, Tameside to parents Charles Hurst, a professional footballer and serving soldier, and Evelyn M Hopkins.

Hurst was an English professional footballer playing at centre-half for various clubs including Bristol Rovers, Oldham Athletic and Rochdale. He started his football career with non-league Hyde United in the mid-1930s before playing for Bristol Rovers (1938–43), Oldham Athletic (1943–46) and Rochdale (1946–47). WWII took the best years of his footballing career, seeing him serve in the British Army. He was among the British Expeditionary Force soldiers rescued during the Dunkirk evacuation in June 1940. After the war finished he returned to play for Oldham and then Rochdale AFC, before moving south. Hurst ended his football career playing non-league football for Chelmsford City and Sudbury Town.

He played in one match for Mossley, scoring a goal in the 1947–48 season, when the family relocated to Chelmsford in Essex. Hurst became Sudbury's player-manager in 1950–51. He took the team to the Suffolk Senior Cup final and third place in the Essex & Suffolk Border League. He also managed non-league side Halstead Town, reportedly giving his 14-year-old son Geoff a game around 1955. After retiring from football he worked as a toolmaker in Essex. Charles Hurst died two days before his 80th birthday in 1999 and his wife Evelyn died the following year in 2000.

Geoff's paternal grandparents – James Edwin Hurst and Fanny Burt

Geoff's paternal grandfather James Edwin Hurst (or Hirst) was born 4th Quarter 1893 in Denton, Lancashire to parents James Jackson Hurst, a stone mason, and Sarah Elizabeth Bailey (Ashton-under-Lyne, 8D/497). In 1911, James Edwin Hurst, 17, a felt hat office clerk, at 61 Manchester Road, Denton, with father James Jackson Hurst, 49, a monumental mason, mother Sarah Elizabeth, 43, a felt hat trimmer, and his 3 brothers.

Geoff's grandmother Fanny Burt (or Bailey) was born illegitimately on 4 January 1893 in Sandbach, Cheshire to reputed father James Burt and mother Mary Jane Bailey. She was registered as Fanny Bailey in 2nd Quarter 1893 (Congleton, 8A/334). She was raised as Fanny Burt and her parents lived in an on-off cohabiting relationship. In 1901,

Fanny, 8, at 37 Astbury Street, Sandbach, with father James Burt, 61, a retired labourer, siblings Frank, 10, Lillie, 6, and Annie, 5. Fanny's father James Burt died in 1908. In 1911, Fanny Burt, 19, a laundry machinist, at 58 Manchester Road, Denton, with mother Mary Jane Burt, 58, a widow, at the home of her brother-in-law James Bailey, 37, a fish and fruit dealer, sister-in-law Emma Bailey, 35, and their 2 children.

James Hurst, 22, a greengrocer's salesman, married Fanny Burt, 21, a laundress, both of 58 Manchester Road, Denton, on 16 February 1913. They married in the United Methodist Church, Denton. The wedding was conducted by Rev Arthur Bamforth, Methodist minister; the witnesses were William and Edith Hurst (Ashton-under-Lyne, 8D/835).

Son Charles Hurst, aka Charlie, was born on 25 January 1919 in Denton, Tameside, Lancashire, to parents James Hurst and Fanny Burt (Ashton-under-Lyne, 8C/513). In 1939 War Register, James Hurst, born 6 July 1890, an engineer's transport manager, at 7 Cemetery Road, Denton, with wife Fanny, born 4 January 1893. It is likely their son Charles was there, shown as 'record officially closed', most likely as Charles was engaged in war service.

James E Hurst, 59, died in 1952 in Salford, Lancashire and wife Fanny Hurst nee Burt, 58, died in 1952 in Amounderness, Lancashire.

Geoff's maternal grandparents –
Francis William Hopkins and Louisa Elizabeth Burton Blick

Geoff's maternal grandfather Francis William Hopkins was born on 14 May 1890 in Hawkesbury, Chipping Sodbury, Gloucestershire, near Bristol, to parents Joseph Hopkins, a labourer, and Sarah Bethell. In 1891, Francis W, 10 months old, resided in a cottage in Hawkesbury, Chipping Sodbury, with father Joseph Hopkins, 29, a general labourer, and mother Sarah, 25.

Geoff's grandmother Louise Elizabeth Burton Blick aka Louisa was born illegitimately on 3 March 1895 in Cam, Gloucestershire to parents George Latimer Blick, a fish-monger, and Emily Organ nee Hampton. She was baptized as Louisa Eliza Blick on 5 May 1895 in Lower Cam Parish to parents George Blick, a fishmonger, and Emily Organ. In 1901, Louisa E B, 6, at Cam Street, Cam, with her father George L Blick, 37, a cloth mill wool binder, mother Emma, 37, and her siblings. In 1911, (Louise) Eliza, 16, a cloth manufacturer's cloth picker, at Old Mill, Upper Cam, with father George Blick, 47, a cloth manufacturer's pool blender, mother Emma, 48, and her siblings.

Frances William Hopkins, 25, an iron fettler, married Louise Elizabeth Burton Blick on 2 August 1915, during WWI, in All Saints Church, Gloucester. The wedding was conducted by F R Standfast, assistant curate; the witnesses were Charles W H Sterry and Edwin Joseph Thornhill, as registered in 3rd Quarter 1915 (Gloucester, 6A/853). Daughter Evelyn M Hopkins was born in 1st Quarter 1918 in Cam, Gloucestershire to parents Frances W Hopkins and Louise Blick (Dursley, 6A/373). In 1939 War Register, Francis W Hopkins, born 14 May 1890, an engineer's fitter, at 10 Everlands, Cam, Dursley, with wife Louise, born 3 March 1895, a propeller factory worker. Louise almost certainly worked at the Gloster Aircraft Company factory in Brockworth, Gloucester making propellers for Hawker Hurricanes. Evelyn, a domestic, at The Beeches, Soudley. By 1940, the family lived in Stroud, Gloucestershire, where their daughter Evelyn met and married Private Charles Hurst. Francis William Hopkins, 67, died in 1957 (Stroud, 7B/434).

Geoff's paternal great-grandparents –
James Jackson Hurst and Sarah Elizabeth Bailey

Geoff's great-grandfather James Jackson Hurst (or Hirst) was born around 1862 in Chapel-en-le-Frith, Derbyshire to parents Joseph and Mary A Hurst (or Hirst). Joseph Hurst was born around 1822 in Roberttown, Kirklees and Mary A (Hurst) was born around 1824 in Hightown, Liversedge, both in Yorkshire.

His great-grandmother Sarah Elizabeth Bailey was born around 1868 in Dukinfield, Cheshire to father Benjamin Bailey, a hatter. James Jackson Hurst, 27, a stone mason, of 31 Wilton Street, Denton, married Sarah Elizabeth Bailey, 21, a hat trimmer, of 24 Heaton Street, Denton, on 29 September 1888 in the Methodist New Connexion Chapel, Red Hall, Audenshaw, as conducted by Rev J. W. W. Walls, Methodist minister.

James and Sarah had 6 known children in Denton, although 2 died in infancy; Joseph (b. ~1890), Harry (b. ~1891), James Edwin (b. ~1893) and Herbert (b. ~1896). In 1891, James J Hurst, 29, a stone mason, at 68 Heaton Street,

Denton, with wife Sarah E, 23, a felt hat trimmer, sons Joseph, 1, and Harry, 3 weeks old. Son James Edwin Hurst (or Hirst) was born 4th Quarter 1893 in Denton, Lancashire to parents James Jackson Hurst, a stone mason, and Sarah Elizabeth Bailey (Ashton-under-Lyne, 8D/497).

In 1901, James J Hurst, 39, a stone mason, at 61 Manchester Road, Denton, with wife Sarah E, 33, sons Joseph, 11, Harry, 10, James E, 7, and Herbert, 5. In 1911, James Jackson Hurst, 49, a monumental mason, still resided with wife Sarah Elizabeth, 43, a felt hat trimmer, sons Joseph, 21, a stone mason, Harry, 20, a felt hat warehouseman, James Edwin, 17, and Herbert, 15, both felt hat office clerks. It seems James switched to being a hatter by 1913 as this was recorded as his occupation on his son James's wedding certificate. James Jackson Hurst (or Hirst), 57, died in 1918, during WWI, in Ashton-under-Lyne and his wife Sarah died in the 1930s.

Geoff's paternal great-grandparents – James Burt and Mary Jane Bailey

Geoff's other paternal great-grandfather James Burt was born around 1840 in Biddulph, Staffordshire and his great-grandmother Mary Jane Bailey was born around 1853 in Macclesfield, Cheshire. It appears James Burt and Mary Jane Bailey never married, but lived as husband and wife. They had 4 known children in Sandbach, Cheshire; Frank (b. 4 Q. 1890), Fanny (b. 2 Q. 1893), Lillie (b. 4 Q. 1895) and Annie (b. 4 Q. 1897).

In 1901 James Burt, 61, a retired labourer, at 37 Astbury Street, Sandbach, with children Frank, 10, Fanny, 8, Lillie, 6, and Annie, 5. James Burt, 68, died in 1908 in Sandbach (Congleton, 8A/211). In 1911, Mary Jane Burt, 58, a widow, at 58 Manchester Road, Denton, with her daughter Fanny Burt, 19, a laundry machinist, at the home of her son James Bailey, 37, a fish and fruit dealer, her daughter-in-law Emma Bailey, 35, and their 2 children.

Geoff's maternal great-grandparents – Joseph Hopkins and Sarah Bethell

Geoff's maternal great-grandfather Joseph Hopkins was born around 1862 in Hawkesbury, Gloucestershire to father William Hopkins, a sawyer. His great-grandmother Sarah Bethell was born around 1866 in Horton, Gloucestershire to parents Hester and William Bethell, a labourer. Joseph Hopkins, 27, a labourer, married Sarah Bethell, 23, both in Hawkesbury, in October 1888 in St Mary's Church. The wedding was conducted by W McCarthy; the witnesses were Daniel Bethell, Daniel Davies, Annie Bethell and Hannah Bethell. In 1891, Joseph Hopkins, 29, a general labourer, resided in a cottage in Hawkesbury, Chipping Sodbury, with wife Sarah, 25, and son Francis W, 10 months old.

Geoff's maternal great-grandparents –
George Latimer Blick and Emily Hampton

Geoff's other maternal great-grandfather George Latimer Blick was born around 1864 in Gloucester, Gloucestershire to parents Margaret and Robert William Blick, a labourer, both born around 1836 in Gloucester. In 1871, George Latimer Blick, 7, a scholar, at 3 Union Street, Gloucester, with her father Robert William Blick, 35, a carpenter, joiner and hawker, mother Margaret, 35, and brother, Robert, 4.

It seems the family legend that Geoff's maternal line descended from Germany is based on the Blick surname. Although the surname Blick is common in Germany and Holland, it is also an old Anglo-Saxon surname commonly found in middle England. It derives from the pre-7th century 'blaec', meaning black, and usually describes someone dark-haired or with a swarthy complexion. Robert William Blick's father Charles Blick, a master plasterer, was also born around 1803 in Rodborough, Gloucestershire, with no evidence of German ancestry.

His great-grandmother Emily aka Emma Hampton was born around 1863 in Cam, Gloucestershire to her father John Hampton, a carpenter. Emily Hampton got married to William Thomas Organ in 1883 (Derby, 7B/702). However, by 1888 she cohabited with George Blick.

George and Emma had 8 known children, including Lillian F M (b. ~1889, Gloucester), George (b. ~1892, Gloucester), Louise Elizabeth Burton aka Louisa (b. 3 March 1895, Cam), Emma V (b. ~1898, Slimbridge); in Cam, Edith W (b. ~1900), Robert (b. ~1903) and Dolly (b. ~1906). In 1901,

George L Blick, 37, a cloth mill wool binder, at Cam Street, Cam, with Emma, 37, daughters Lilian F M, 12, Louisa E B, 6, Emma V, 3, and Edith W, 9 months old.

On 21 October 1905, after many years living together, George Latimer Blick, 41, an unmarried labourer, married long-term partner Emma Organ nee Hampton, 43, a widow, both of Dainty Street, Gloucester, in St James Church. The wedding was conducted by Rev H Edward Billett; the witnesses were Frank Oliver Mitchell and Elizabeth Burton Blick., Daughter Louise was named after her.

In 1911, George Blick, 47, a pool blender for a cloth manufacturer, at Old Mill, Upper Cam, with wife Emma, 48, children Lilly, 22, a cloth picker, George, 19, a comb grinder in a sheep shearing works, Eliza (Louise), 16, a cloth manufacturer's cloth picker, Emma, 13, Edith, 10, Robert, 8, and Dolly, 5, all at school. Also boarding at George's home was Joseph Thornhill, 22, a comb grinder in a sheep shearing works, wife Florence, 23, daughter Valentine, 3, and a new born infant.

CHAPTER 10

Martin Peters MBE (inside left)

Honours as an England player:

1 FIFA World Cup 1966

1 EUFA European Championship (Bronze medallist) 1968

M artin Stanford Peters MBE was born on 8 November 1943, during WWII, at Egham Road, off Beckton Road, Plaistow, Essex to parents William Stanford Peters, a Thames lighterman, and Mary Margaret Brown (West Ham, 4A/174). Shortly after his birth Peters was evacuated with his mother Mary to Shropshire to avoid the London Blitz by the German Luftwaffe. Around 1950, when he was seven, his family moved to Dagenham, Essex where he attended Fanshawe School.

At school, he played centre-half and full-back. He caught the attention of Fulham, Arsenal, Tottenham Hotspur and Chelsea. Peters did not support any particular club as a schoolboy, although he favoured joining Chelsea, as his friend Terry Venables, who he played with at Dagenham Schoolboys, had signed for Chelsea. After playing for England schoolboys he was scouted by Wally St Pier for West Ham United. In the summer of 1959 he signed as a 15-year-old apprentice with the Hammers.

He was an English professional footballer and manager. As a member of the England team that won the 1966 World Cup, he famously scored the second of England's four goals in the final against West Germany. He also won a bronze medal with England at the 1968 European Championships in Italy and played in the 1970 World Cup finals in Mexico. Peters played club football for West Ham United, Tottenham Hotspur, Norwich City and Sheffield United.

Peters was known as 'the complete midfielder' as he could pass the ball well with either foot. He was effective in the air and difficult to mark due to his movement. A free kick specialist, he was described by England manager Sir Alf Ramsey, after a game against Scotland in 1968, as being *"ten years ahead of his time"*. His versatility was such that, while at West Ham, he played every position in the team. This included goalkeeper in his third game, replacing injured Brian Rhodes. Alongside England teammates Bobby Moore and Geoff Hurst, Peters won the European Cup Winners' Cup in 1965 at Wembley with the Hammers beating 1860 Munich. Transferred from West Ham United to Tottenham Hotspur in 1970, he became Britain's first £200,000 footballer. He won the UEFA Cup in 1972 when Spurs beat Wolverhampton Wanderers in the first all-English European final. He briefly managed Sheffield United before retiring in 1981.

Martin's parents –
William Stanford Peters and Mary Margaret Brown

Martin's father William Stanford Peters was born on 7 May 1912 and baptized on 7 June 1912 in St Matthias Church, Mafeking Road, Canning Town, Essex to parents Stanford John Peters and Daisy Marie Hawkes (West Ham, 4A/232). After leaving school, William became a Thames lighterman, working on long flat-bottomed freight barges plying the busy River Thames. The lightermen were highly regarded in the London docks community and traced their esteemed occupation back to Henry VIII's reign. As ships increased in size and could no longer pass upstream at London Bridge, lightermen transported goods to and from the busy lower Thames docklands.

A couple of weeks into WWI, Martin's mother Mary Margaret Brown was born on 29 August 1914 to parents Albert Thomas Brown and Mary Elizabeth Stuart (West Ham, 4A/446). She was baptized on 13 September 1914 in St Magdalene's Church, East Ham, Essex William Stanford Peters, a Thames lighterman, married Mary Margaret Brown in 1st Quarter 1937 (West Ham, 4A/237).

In 1939 War Register, William S Peters, born 7 May 1912, a general cargo lighterman, at 15 Botha Road, off Egham Road, West Ham, with wife Mary M, born 29 August 1914, a waitress. The record also shows Mary was placed on a 'special posting' in war service around the corner on Egham Road, 'record officially closed'.

Son Martin Stanford Peters was born on 8 November 1943 at Egham Road, off Beckton Road, Plaistow to parents William S Peters, a Thames lighterman, and Mary M Brown in 4th Quarter 1943 (West Ham, 4A/174). Shortly after their son Martin's birth, Mary was evacuated with her son to Shropshire to avoid the London Blitz bombing by the German Luftwaffe. Around 1950, the Peters family moved to Dagenham, Essex. William Stanford Peters, 77, died in 1989 in Brentwood, Essex. His wife Mary Margaret Peters nee Brown, 83, died in 1997 in Brentwood.

Martin's paternal grandparents –
Stanford John Peters and Daisy Marie Hawkes

Martin's paternal grandfather Stanford John Peters aka Stamford was born in 3rd Quarter 1890 in Plaistow, Essex to parents William Henry Peters, a tug boat engine driver, and Alice Legon (West Ham, 4A/76). In 1891, Stanford J, 10 months old, at 119 Star Lane, Plaistow with father William Henry Peters, 42, a boat engine driver, mother Alice, 37, and his siblings.

Martin's grandmother Daisy Marie Hawkes (or Hawks) was born in 2nd Quarter 1891 to parents Alfred Hawkes and Maria Reader in Grays, Essex (Orsett, 4A/449). In 1901, Daisy, 9, at 12 Globe Terrace, Grays Thurrock, with father

Alfred Hawkes, 48, a barge lighterman, mother Maria, 47, and her siblings. In 1911, Stanford, 24, a Thames lighterman, resided in West Ham, Canning Town, with father Henry Peters, 63, a tug engine driver for the Port of London Authority, mother Alice, 48, and her sister Rose, 25, who was recorded as 'deaf and dumb'.

Later that year, Stanford John Peters married Daisy Marie Hawkes in St Matthias Church, Canning Town on 6 November 1911 (West Ham, 4A/31). Son William Stanford Peters was born on 5 June 1912 in Plaistow to parents Stanford John Peters and Daisy Marie Hawkes (West Ham, 4A/232). Daughter Daisy Marie Alice Peters was born on 8 October 1913 at 161 Star Lane, Canning Town. However, aged 4, she died on 10 December 1917. Just six days later Daisy Peters faced further tragedy.

On 1 October 1915, during WWI, Stanford John Peters, a lighterman, enlisted as Sapper 122226 Royal Engineers, Inland Water Transport. After being bombarded in France, he was returned to Western Heights Hospital, Dover, Kent. He died on active service, at 7.50pm on 16 December 1917, of a tremor on the brain. Stanford's personal effects were meticulously recorded including a writing tablet, four pence in cash and his lighterman licence. The death of Stanford John Peters, 27, was registered in 4th Quarter 1917 (Dover, 2A/1342). He is commemorated on Panel 2 of the Brookwood 1914-18 Memorial in Brookwood Military Cemetery, Pirbright, Surrey.

Martin's maternal grandparents –
Albert Thomas Brown and Mary Elizabeth Stuart

Martin's paternal grandfather Albert Thomas Brown was born on 23 March 1886 in Dalston, Hackney, London. Martin's grandmother Mary Elizabeth Stuart was born on 21 December 1890 at Queenwood Lodge, Ottershaw, Surrey to Scottish parents George Frater Stuart, an estate gardener, and mother Elizabeth Marshall Swan (Chertsey, 2A/47). Mary was baptized on 1 March 1891 in Christ Church, Guildford Road, Ottershaw. In 1891, Mary, 3 months old, at Queenwood Lodge, Queenwood Estate, Ottershaw, Chertsey, with father George Stuart, 43, an estate gardener, mother Eliza, 35, and her siblings.

Albert Thomas Brown married Mary Elizabeth Stuart in 4th Quarter 1909 (West Ham, 4A/552). Albert and Mary had 4 known children in East Ham; Albert Thomas Jr. (b. 22 May 1910), George A (b. 26 May 1912), Mary Margaret (b. 29 August 1914) and Stanley S (b. 21 July 1919).

In 1911, Albert Brown, 26, a machine ruler in a stationer's firm, at 9 Burges Road, East Ham, with wife Mary, 23, and son Albert, 10 months old. Daughter Mary Margaret Brown was born on 29 August 1914 and baptized on 13 September 1914 in St Magdalene's Church, East Ham to parents Albert Thomas Brown and Mary Elizabeth Stuart (West Ham, 4A/446). Given the gaps in births between 1914 and 1919, it suggests Albert Thomas Brown served in WWI.

In 1939 War Register, Albert T Brown, born 23 March 1886, a machine ruler, at 23 St Bernard's Road, East Ham, with wife Mary E, born 21 December 1890, doing unpaid domestic duties, children Albert T Jr., born 22 May 1910, a laundry man and plumber's mate, attached to an Air Raid Precautions Rescue Party, George A, born 26 May 1912, a bank messenger, Stanley S, born 21 July 1919, a general labourer doing heavy work, and a boarder John Everett, born 24 January 1868, another general labourer doing heavy work. Mary Elizabeth Brown nee Stuart, 70, died in 1958 (East Ham, 5A/25). Albert T Brown, 79, died in 1965 (West Ham, 5A/694).

Martin's paternal great-grandparents – William Henry Peters and Alice Legon

Martin's paternal great-grandfather William Henry Peters aka Henry was born around 1848 in Shadwell, Stepney, Middlesex to his father also named William Henry Peters. His great-grandmother Alice Legon was born around 1853 in St George's, Stepney to her father James William Legon. Henry Peters, 26, a mariner, of 2 Golds Hill, Shadwell, married Alice Legon, 21, of 42 Anchor Hope Alley, Wapping, on 3 December 1874 in St Thomas Church, Stepney. Henry's father William Henry Peters, a mariner, was dead by 1874, although Alice's father James William Legon, a lighterman, was still alive.

Henry and Alice had 6 known children in Plaistow, Essex; Alice M (b. ~1877), William Henry (b. ~1880), James A (b. ~1884), Rose Anna (b. 1 Q. 1886, 'deaf and dumb'), Thomas C (b. ~1888) and Stanford John (b. 3 Q. 1890). Son Stanford

John Peters was born in 3rd Quarter 1890 in Plaistow to parents William Henry Peters, a tug boat engine driver, and Alice Legon (West Ham, 4A/76).

In 1891, William Henry Peters, 42, a boat engine driver, at 119 Star Lane, Plaistow, with wife Alice, 37, children Alice M, 14, an apprentice dressmaker, William H, 11, James A, 7, Rose A, 5, Thomas C, 3, and Stanford J, 10 months old. In 1911, Henry Peters, 63, a tug engine driver for the Port of London Authority, resided in West Ham, Canning Town with wife Alice, 48, son Stanford, 24, a Thames lighterman, and daughter Rose, 25. William Henry Peters, 67, died in 1915 (West Ham, 4A/118A). Alice Peters nee Legon died in 1935 (Billericay, Essex, 4A/649).

Martin's paternal great-grandparents – Alfred Hawkes and Maria Reader

Martin's other paternal great-grandfather Alfred Hawkes was born in 1st Quarter 1852 in Orsett, Essex and his great-grandmother Maria Reader was born around 1854 in Grays, Essex. Alfred and Maria had 10 known children in Grays; William A (b. ~1874), Minnie J (b. ~1877, died in infancy), Gertrude E (b. ~1879, died in infancy), Edward (b. ~1881), Harry (b. ~1883), Fred (b. ~1886), Gladys (b. ~1889), Daisy Marie (b. 2 Q. 1891), Stanley (b. ~1894) and Vera (b. ~1898). In 1881, Alfred Hawkes, 27, a waterman, at 6 Victoria Terrace, Grays Thurrock, with wife Maria, 27, children William A, 7, a scholar, Minnie J, 4, a scholar, and

Gertrude E, 2. Daughter Daisy Marie Hawkes (or Hawks) was born in 2nd Quarter 1891 to parents Alfred Hawkes and Maria Reader in Grays Thurrock (Orsett, 4A/449).

In 1901, Alfred Hawkes, 48, a barge lighterman, at 12 Globe Terrace, Grays Thurrock, with wife Maria, 47, children William, 27, a ship's fireman, Edward, 20, Harry, 18, Fred, 15, both bargemen, Gladys, 12, Daisy, 9, Stanley, 7, and Vera, 3. They also had a visitor Anna Judd, 19, a domestic servant. Maria Hawkes, 47, died a few months later in 1901 in Orsett, Essex. Alfred Hawkes, 59, died in 1922 in Barnet, London.

Martin's maternal great-grandparents – George Frater Stuart and Elizabeth Marshall Swan

Martin's maternal great-grandfather George Frater Stuart (or Stewart) was born in 2nd Quarter 1844 in North Eglingham, Northumberland (Glendale, 25/259), although later raised in the newly formed Free Church of Scotland faith in Melrose, Roxburghshire, to parents James Stuart, a gardener, (b. ~1798, Berwickshire) and Mary Frater (b. ~1801, Roxburghshire). George's father was an estate gardener at Eglingham Hall, owned by the Barons Ogle of Ogle for 400 years.

In 1851, George, 6, at Middle Steads, Bolton, Northumberland, with father James Stuart, 53, a gardener, mother Mary, 50, siblings Thomas, 24, an agricultural labourer, Christina, 17, a household worker, Susan, 11, and Hannah, 9. In 1861, George, 16, a gardener, at Free Church Place, Melrose, with father James Stewart, 62, a gardener, and mother Mary, 60. Three doors along stood Melrose Academy, a boarding school at 5 Free Church Place, run by the Free Church. It was built in 1844, the year after the Great Disruption, and is now a Category C Listed Building.

Martin's great-grandmother Elizabeth Marshall Swan was born on 2 May 1855 in Knowehead, Cardross, Dunbartonshire, to parents John Swan and Annie McMoodie Rankin. George Frater Stuart, 33, a jobbing estate gardener, of 17 Johnston Street, Greenock, married Elizabeth Marshall Swan, 25, of Margaret Street, Greenock, at Collin's Land, Langloan, Old Monkland, Lanarkshire, on 9 December 1880 according to the Free Church of Scotland forms. The wedding was conducted by Rev Alexander Ogilvy, minister of Free Middle Church, Coatbridge; the best man was James Hunter Crawford and the best maid was Christina Swan, Elizabeth's sister.

On 22 December 1881, George's widowed mother Mary Stuart nee Frater, 81, died at 17 Johnston Street, Greenock, of paralysis. This was certified by Dr James Whiteford MD and registered by her daughter Hannah Stuart on 28 December 1881 at Greenock Registry Office. Mary's parents were Thomas Frater, a farmer, and Isabella Waddell.

George and Eliza moved south to Balham, Surrey, where George worked as an estate gardener. George and Eliza had 4 known children; Annie (b. ~1882, Balham), James (b. ~1887, Henley), Mary Elizabeth (b. 21 December 1890,

Ottershaw) and Isabella S (b. 3 November 1897, Habergham Eaves, Burnley).

In 1891, George Stuart, 43, an estate gardener, at Queenwood Lodge, Queenwood Estate, Ottershaw, Chertsey, with wife Eliza, 35, children Annie, 9, a scholar, James, 4, and Mary, 3 months old. Ottershaw lies in the historic borough of Runnymede. This is the famous site of the Magna Carta signing between King John and the barons on 15 June 1215.

The Great Charter of Freedom concludes with these words:

> *"Given by Our hand in the meadow which is called Runnymede between Windsor and Staines, on the fifteenth day of June in the Seventeenth year of Our Reign".*

The Queenwood Estate was a large privately-owned agricultural estate, the proprietor being the author and naturalist Mr R H Otter J.P., who published *Winters Abroad: Intended for the use of invalids, 1882*. Queenwood is now an American-owned exclusive private golf club.

From 1897 until 1901, the family lived in Habergham Eaves village, Burnley, Lancashire. In 1909 they moved back south to Essex, where George was now a land steward on the Bower House estate, Orange Tree Hill, in historic Havering-atte-Bower. The Bower House and stable block is a Grade I listed Palladian mansion in Havering-atte-Bower. It was built in 1729 by Henry Flitcroft. It incorporated architectural features salvaged from the ruined Havering

Palace, dating back to Edward the Confessor and later King Harold, who was defeated by William the Conqueror in 1066. The Bower House remained a private home until 1976, when it was purchased by Ford Motor Corporation. It is now a Christian training centre.

In 1911, George Frater Stuart, 64, a land steward, at North Lodge, Havering-atte-Bower, Essex, with wife Elizabeth Marshall Stuart, 54, children Annie, 29, a sick nurse, James, 24, an estate clerk of works, and Isabella S, 13, a scholar. George Frater Stuart, 82, died in 1926 at Brookside, Ongar, Essex. In 1939 War Register, Elizabeth M Stuart, born 2 May 1855, an incapacitated widow, at Brookside, Ongar with her unmarried daughter Isabella S Stuart, born 3 November 1897, a school teacher. Elizabeth Marshall Stuart nee Swan died in 1944 in Wandsworth, London.

Martin's maternal great-great-grand-grandparents – John Swan and Annie McMoodie Rankin

Martin's maternal great-great-grandfather John Swan, his mother's maiden name Marshall, was born around 1820 in Cardross, Dunbartonshire, Scotland. In 1841, John Swan, 20, a male servant, at Wallaceton Barn, Cardross, on the Kilmahew Estate, owned by James Burns of Bloomhill.

A mansion, built in 1865–1868, was originally the home of James Burns and his son John, then later the Allan family from the early 20th century until just after WWII. The estate was sold in 1948 to the Roman Catholic Archdiocese of Glasgow. Architects Gillespie, Kidd & Coia employees Isi Metzstein and Andy MacMillan developed a radical design, with the mansion becoming professorial accommodation. Around it they wrapped a striking main block, a convent block, a sanctuary block and a classroom block. The old mansion became one side of a quadrangle, creating a juxtaposition between the old and new buildings.

It opened in 1961 as St Peter's Roman Catholic Seminary in Cardross. Although now in a ruinous state, it is described by the international architecture conservation organisation DOCOMOMO as a modern 'building of world significance'. It is one of only 42 post-war buildings in Scotland to be listed at Category A, the highest level of protection for a building of 'special architectural or historic interest'.

Martin's great-great-grandmother Ann McMoodie Rankin aka Annie was born around 1824 in Old Monkland, Lanarkshire, to parents Robert Rankin and Isabella Selkirk, both born around 1788.

John Swan, an agricultural labourer, married Ann Rankin in July 1846 in Cardross Church. As was customary, the couple posted the marriage banns in their respective parishes. On 3 July 1846 'John and Anne', travelled to the parish of Bonhill, where Ann was living and working, to post the banns. The following day, on 4 July 1846, 'John and Ann' returned to Cardross Church. After three Sabbaths announcing the banns, John and Ann married.

In 1851, John Swan, 31, an agricultural labourer, at Kippoch Offices, Cardross, with wife Ann, 27, children

David B, 3, Isabella S, 1, and Robert, 1 month old. John and Ann had two other daughters, Elizabeth Marshall Swan (b. 1855, Knowehead, Cardross) and Christina. John Swan, 54, a house factor for the Kilmahew Estate, died in 1874 in Cardross. Annie McMoodie Swan nee Rankin, 79, died in 1903 in Coatbridge, Old Monkland.

CHAPTER 11

Roger Hunt MBE (outside left)

Honours as an England player:
1 FIFA World Cup 1966

Roger Hunt MBE was born on 20 July 1938 in Glazebury, Leigh, Lancashire, to parents Richard Hunt, a haulage contractor, and Ellen Jacklin (Leigh, 8C/321). Hunt attended Culcheth County School and Leigh Grammar. In his schooldays he played for Croft Youth Club, and then non-league clubs Devizes Town in Wiltshire, during his national service, followed by Stockton Heath. He was signed for Liverpool by manager Phil Taylor in July 1958. Hunt made his debut and scored his first goal for the club on 9 September 1959. This was in a Second Division fixture at Anfield against Scunthorpe United. After legendary manager Bill Shankly replaced Taylor, the burly Scot from Glenbuck and his 'Boot Room' staff embarked upon a clear out of 24 players. However, Hunt was retained and was a major factor in the Reds' success in the 1960s. This began the rise of the Anfield club into a European and world powerhouse.

Eleven years with Liverpool, he was the club's record goal-scorer with 286 goals, until overtaken by Ian Rush. Nonetheless, Hunt remains Liverpool's record league goal-scorer with 244 goals. Under Bill Shankly, Hunt won two league titles and an FA Cup. In August 1964 he also scored the first ever goal seen on BBC's Match of the Day. Regarded as one of Liverpool's greatest players, Hunt was nicknamed 'Sir Roger' by the club's fans. He ranked 13th on the '100 Players Who Shook the Kop'.

Hunt was capped 34 times for England, with his debut given by manager Walter Winterbottom, while still a Second Division player. This was on 4 April 1962 in a friendly against Austria at Wembley. He scored on his international debut as England won 3–1. He was part of the England squad at the 1962 World Cup in Chile, although not selected.

England hosted the 1966 World Cup, and Hunt, along with Liverpool teammates Ian Callaghan and Gerry Byrne, was selected by manager Alf Ramsey for the 22-man squad. Hunt was one of three forwards selected for the tournament. He initially partnered Spurs striker Jimmy Greaves up front, however, following a serious leg injury to Greaves he played alongside Geoff Hurst of West Ham. He played in all six games, scoring three times, twice against France and once against Mexico. England won the Jules Rimet trophy after a 4–2 extra-time win over West Germany in the final at Wembley.

He signed for Bolton Wanderers in December 1969. In 1971, he moved on loan to Hellenic FC in South Africa's National Football League. He retired in 1972, and had a testimonial with Liverpool in April 1972, attended by 56,000 fans. After retiring from football, he joined his brother Peter, in taking over Hunt Brothers, as the third generation of the family-run haulage business. It was established by Richard and Harry Hunt in 1929. Hunt was inducted into the English Football Hall of Fame in 2006.

Roger's parents –
Richard Hunt and Ellen Jacklin

Roger's father Richard Hunt was born on 8 February 1913 in Rixton, Lancashire to parents Richard Hunt and Annie Hepherd (Warrington, 8C/495). Roger's mother Ellen Jacklin was born on 15 August 1912 in Glazebury, Lancashire to parents Edward Jacklin and Ellen Ashworth (Leigh, 8C/497). In 1921, Ellen, 8, a scholar, resided in Culcheth village with father Edward Jacklin, 37, mother Ellen, 38, and his brother Edward, 10, a scholar.

Along with his brother, Harry Hunt, Richard co-founded Hunt Brothers haulage firm in 1929 based in Culcheth, Warrington. Richard Hunt, a haulage contractor, married Ellen Jacklin in 3rd Quarter 1937 (Leigh, 8C/659). The following year, son Roger Hunt was born on 20 July 1938 in

Glazebury to parents Richard Hunt, a haulage contractor, and Ellen Jacklin (Leigh, 8C/321).

In 1939 War Register, Richard Hunt, born 8 February 1913, a heavy lorry motor haulage contractor, at 167 Warrington Road, Colborne, with wife Ellen, born 15 August 1912, doing unpaid domestic duties, and son Roger, born 20 July 1938, under school age. Ellen's older brother Edward Jacklin and wife Zillah lived next door at No.165.

Richard and Ellen also had a son Peter Hunt born in 2nd Quarter 1940 (Leigh, 8C/560). Peter Hunt followed his father Richard into the family haulage business at Hunt Brothers. His brother, Roger, also joined the company after retiring in 1972 from his football career.

Roger's paternal grandparents – Richard Hunt and Annie Hepherd

Roger's paternal grandfather Richard Hunt was born on 18 June 1872 in Deane, Bolton, Lancashire, to parents Henry Hunt, an innkeeper, and Hannah Pendlebury. Richard was baptized on 4 August 1872 in St Mary's Church, Deane by T M Knowles, curate. In 1881, Richard, 8, a scholar, at Irlam Moss, Barton-upon-Irwell, with father Henry Hunt, 37, a farmer, and his family. In 1891, Richard, 18, a farmer's son, at Glazebrook Lane, Rixton-with-Glazebrook, with father Henry Hunt, 47, a farmer, mother Hannah, 51, and his siblings. They still lived there in 1901.

Roger's grandmother Annie Hepherd aka Ann was born on 11 November 1877 in Woolston village, Lancashire to parents James Hepherd, a farmer's son, and Alice Daintith (Warrington, 8C/230). In 1881, Ann, 3, at Dam Lane, Woolston, with father James Hepherd, a farmer, mother Alice, 21, and her siblings. In 1891, Ann, 13, a scholar, at Manchester Road, Woolston, with father James Hepherd, 41, a farmer, mother Alice, 31, and her siblings.

Richard Hunt, 35, a farmer, married Annie Hepherd, 29, on 4 December 1907 in Padgate (Warrington, 8C/274). Richard and Annie had 3 known children in Rixton; Henry aka Harry (b. ~1908), Gertrude (b. ~1910) and Richard (b. 8 February 1913). In 1911, Richard Hunt, 38, a farmer, at Dam Lane, Rixton, with wife Annie, 32, son Henry, 3, and daughter Gertrude, 1. Son Richard Hunt was born on 8 February 1913 in Rixton to parents Richard Hunt, a farmer, and Annie Hepherd (Warrington, 8C/495).

Richard Hunt, 55, a farmer, died on 21 May 1927 in Leigh, Lancashire. Richard was buried alongside his parents Henry and Hannah Hunt in Hollinfare Cemetery, Rixton-with-Glazebrook. Annie Hunt nee Hepherd, only 52, died on 13 October 1929 in Rixton and was buried alongside her husband in Hollinfare Cemetery.

Roger's maternal grandparents –
Edward Jacklin and Ellen Ashworth

Roger's maternal grandfather Edward Jacklin was born on 10 October 1884 in Salford, Lancashire to his father Edward Jacklin, a labourer. Roger's grandmother Ellen Ashworth was born on 25 June 1882 in Pendleton, Lancashire to her father William Henry Ashworth, an engineer. Edward Jacklin, 22, a signalman, of 84 Tootal Drive, Salford, married Ellen Ashworth, 24, of 25 Derby Avenue, Salford, on 17 August 1907. The wedding in St Luke's Church, Salford was conducted by Rev C P Wilson, vicar; the best man was John Henry Ashworth and the best maid was Sarah Emma Collins.

Edward and Ellen had 3 known children; Bertha (b. ~1908), Edward (b. ~1910) and daughter Ellen Jacklin was born in 4th Quarter 1913 in Glazebury (Leigh, 8E/475). In 1911, Edward Jacklin, 26, a railway signalman for the London & North Western Railway Company, at 112 Warrington Road, Glazebury, with wife Ellen, 27, children Bertha, 3, and Edward, 2 months old. In 1921, Edward Jacklin, 37, a signalman, resided in Culcheth, with wife Ellen, 38, son Edward, 10, and daughter Ellen, 8, both scholars. In 1923, Edward, a signalman, was transferred to the newly amalgamated London Midland & Scottish Railway Company.

In 1939 War Register, Edward Jacklin, born 10 October 1884, a railway signalman on the LMS, at 16 Bradburn Grove, Eccles, Greater Manchester, with wife Ellen, born 25 June 1882, doing unpaid domestic duties. In 1947, Edward transferred to the nationalised British Railway Company.

Edward Jacklin, 76, died in 1961 (Salford, 10F/699). Ellen Jacklin nee Ashworth, 80, died in 1964 (Leigh, 10D/31).

Roger's paternal great-grandparents – Henry Hunt and Hannah Pendlebury

Roger's paternal great-grandfather Henry Hunt aka Harry was born around 1844 in Much Hoole, Lancashire. Around 4 years earlier in 1840, Gordon Banks' great-grandfather Thomas Scowcroft Banks was also born in Much Hoole. It is incredible to think that a tiny village with a population of less than 400 in the 1840s produced the paternal progenitors of two World Cup winners. Roger's great-grandmother Hannah Pendlebury was born around 1840 in Deane, Bolton, Lancashire.

Henry Hunt married Hannah Pendlebury in 2nd Quarter 1871 (Bolton, 8C/365). Henry and Hannah had 5 known children; in Deane, Richard (b. 18 June 1872), Hannah (b. ~1874); in Blackrod, Alice (b. ~1876), Henry aka Harry (b. ~1878) and Florence (b. ~1880). Richard Hunt was born on 18 June 1872 in Deane, Bolton, Lancashire, to parents Henry Hunt, an innkeeper, and Hannah Pendlebury. Richard was baptized on 4 August 1872 in St Mary's Church, Deane by T M Knowles, curate. Henry was the landlord of the Tempest's Arms, Heaton, Bolton.

In 1881, Henry Hunt, 37, a farmer of 25 acres employing 2 labourers, at Irlam Moss, Barton-upon-Irwell, Lancashire, with his family and servants. In 1891, Henry Hunt, 47, a farmer, at Glazebrook Lane, Rixton-with-Glazebrook, Lancashire, with wife Hannah, 51, children Richard, 18, a farmer's son, Hannah, 17, Alice, 15, Harry, 13, Florence, 11, and Henry's older brother Richard Hunt, 54, an agricultural labourer. Henry and Hannah still farmed there in 1901. Henry Hunt, 63, a farmer, died on 17 January 1908. His wife Hannah, 80, died on 17 December 1920, both in Rixton, and they were buried in Hollinfare Cemetery.

Roger's paternal great-grandfather – James Hepherd and Alice Daintith

Roger's other paternal great-grandfather James Hepherd was born around 1849 in Woolston, Lancashire to parents James and Ann Hepherd. In 1861, James Hepherd, 12, a farmer's son, at Woolston, Rixton, with father James Hepherd, 50, a farmer of 50 acres with 2 men and a boy, (b. ~1811, Woolston), mother Ann, 51, (b. ~1810, Latchford, Cheshire) and his siblings.

Roger's great-grandmother Alice Daintith was born in 2nd Quarter 1860 in Croft (Warrington, 8C/123). James Hepherd married Alice Daintith in 4th Quarter 1875 (Warrington, 8C/205). James and Alice had 7 known children in Woolston; William (b. ~1874, illegitimate), Annie aka Ann (b. 11 November 1877), Sarah (b. ~1880), Alice (b. ~1882), James (b. ~1884), Elizabeth (b. ~1888) and Joseph (b. ~1889).

In 1881, James Hepherd, 31, a farmer of 30 acres employing 3 men and 1 boy, at Dam Lane, Woolston, with wife Alice, 21, a farmer's wife, children William, 4, a scholar, Ann, 3, and Sarah, 1. Also living there were Uncle Thomas Hepherd, 68, a retired farmer, James Frankinson, 32, George Howarth, 15, both indoor farm servants, and Margaret Pemberton, 24, a general domestic servant. In 1891, James Hepherd, 41, a farmer, at Manchester Road, Woolston, with wife Alice, 31, children William, 14, a farmer's son, Ann, 13, Sarah, 11, Alice, 9, James, 7, all scholars, Elizabeth, 3, Joseph, 2, and niece Elizabeth Daintith, 18, a general domestic servant.

Alice Hepherd nee Daintith, 58, died on 22 April 1918, during WWI, and James Hepherd, 79, a farmer, died on 2 April 1928, both in Warrington and are buried in Christ Church graveyard, Padgate, Warrington.

CHAPTER 12

The Other England squad players – World Cup finals 1966

Goalkeepers

12. Ron Springett, Sheffield Wednesday, born 22 July 1935, Fulham, London

13. Peter Bonetti, Chelsea, born 27 September 1941, Putney, London

Defenders

14. Jimmy Armfield, Blackpool, born 21 September 1935, Denton, Lancashire

15. Gerry Byrne, Liverpool, born 29 August 1938, Liverpool, Lancashire

18. Norman Hunter, Leeds United, born 29 October 1943, Eighton Banks, Gateshead, Northumberland

Midfielders

20. Ian Callaghan, Liverpool, born 10 April 1942, Toxteth, Liverpool

17. Ron Flowers, Wolverhampton Wanderers, born 28 July 1934, Edlington, Doncaster, Yorkshire

Forwards

11. John Connelly, Manchester United, born 18 July 1938, St Helens, Lancashire

22. George Eastham, Blackpool, born 21 September 1935, Blackpool, Lancashire

8. Jimmy Greaves, Tottenham Hotspur, born 20 February 1940, Manor Park, Essex

19. Terry Paine, Southampton, born 23 March 1939, Winchester, Hampshire

CHAPTER 13

Sir Alfred Ernest Ramsey (manager)

Honours as an England player / manager:
1 FIFA World Cup 1966
1 EUFA European Championship (Bronze medallist) 1968
6 British Home Championships

S ir Alfred Ernest Ramsey was born on 22 January 1920 at 6 Parrish Cottages, Halbutt Street, Dagenham, still a predominantly agricultural village in Essex (Romford, 4A/1329). Ramsey was the third of six children born to his father Herbert Ramsey, a manual labourer and council dustman, and his mother Florence Bixby. His sister Winnie died in childhood. Parrish Cottages where Ramsey was raised had the most primitive of amenities. Phil Cairns, a childhood friend of Alf, stated that the Ramsey house was *"little more than a wooden hut"*.

Aged five, Ramsey attended Becontree Heath School, with around 200 pupils. The brothers had to walk two hours from their house to get there. They passed a football between each other to break the monotony. A friend Fred Tibble described Ramsey as *"a very quiet boy who really loved sport"*. He was selected to play for Becontree Heath School when he was seven, playing inside-left alongside boys as old as fourteen. His nine-year-old brother Len was inside-right. Two years later, aged nine, Ramsey became captain of the school team.

Ramsey played for Dagenham and Essex County schools teams, and trialled unsuccessfully for the London schools team while at Becontree. On leaving school in 1934, the 14-year-old Ramsey applied for a job at the new Ford Dagenham factory. He then told his family he intended to become a greengrocer. To that end, he became an apprentice at the local Co-operative branch, delivering groceries on a bicycle. The manual work helped bulk up Ramsey's physique. After a two-year hiatus, he returned to football in 1936, joining amateur club Five Elms.

The following year, during the 1937–38 season, Ramsey was spotted by Ned Liddell, a Portsmouth scout. However, after posting the signing-on forms, he heard nothing from the club. He spent the next two years working for the Co-op and playing amateur cricket and football. In 1939 War Register, Alfred E, born 22 January 1920, a grocery shop assistant, still at 6 Parrish Cottages, Halbutt Street, Dagenham, with father Herbert H Ramsey, born 31 January 1890, a dustman doing heavy work, mother Florence, born 10 July 1895, doing unpaid domestic duties, and his brothers.

After the outbreak of WWII in September 1939, Ramsey was conscripted into the British Army on 24 June 1940. He was assigned to the 6th Duke of Cornwall's Light Infantry and did his basic training in Truro. He and other recruits were billeted in a hotel commandeered by the army. Ramsey spent the entire war in Britain on home defence duties. The training was still physically demanding and he stated, *"It made me a fitter young fellow than when I reported for duty as a grocery apprentice from Dagenham"*.

Ramsey rose to company quartermaster sergeant in an anti-aircraft unit. Military service allowed Ramsey to play football more regularly and at a higher standard. In late 1940 he was posted to St Austell, on the south coast of Cornwall. He manned beach defences and became captain of the battalion's football team.

After three years in various seaside postings, in 1943, Ramsey was transferred to Barton Stacey, Hampshire. His commandant Colonel Fletcher was also an accomplished footballer. Ramsey's battalion team featured players from various Football League clubs, including Brentford forward Len Townsend and Arsenal forward Cyril Hodges. Ramsey played at centre-half for his battalion team as Southampton defeated them 10–3 at the Dell in a pre-season friendly on 21 August 1943. A week later, he played again as the battalion took on Southampton's reserves and won the match 4–1.

On 8 October 1943, Colonel Fletcher called Ramsey to his office to inform him Southampton needed a centre-half for their first-team match away to Luton Town. Ramsey replied, *"I'll give it a try, sir."* He signed for Southampton as an amateur, making his debut at Luton's Kenilworth Road ground. He played in three more matches for the team during the 1943–44 season before his battalion's posting to County Durham forced his absence. After his unit returned to the south coast at the start of the 1944–45 season Southampton offered him a professional contract on wages of £2 per match.

After a spell in Occupied Palestine, Ramsey was demobbed in 1946. He formally signed as a professional player for around £6 a week. He played club football for Southampton and White Hart Lane for Tottenham Hotspur. He was in the Spurs side that won the English League championship in 1950–51. He also represented the England national team and captained the side. He played in defence in England's 1950 World Cup squad in Chile. His temporary visa card issued by the 'Republica do Brasil' on 15 June 1950 in London is still on record, allowing him to travel to Chile. He still lived at 6 Parrish Cottages with Herbert and Florence and his profession was 'jugador de futebol'.

In 1955, Ramsey retired from playing aged 35, becoming manager of Ipswich Town in the third tier of English football. Ipswich rose through the divisions winning the Third Division South in 1956–57 and the Second Division in 1960–61. In the 1961–62 season, Ipswich's first campaign in the First Division, Ramsey's team defied all expectations to become English champions.

Ramsey took charge of the England team a year later. He is best known for his time as England manager from 1963 to 1974. This includes managing them to victory in the 1966 World Cup at Wembley. Knighted by Queen Elizabeth II in 1967 in recognition of the World Cup win, Ramsey also managed his country to third place in the 1968 European Championship. He also reached the quarter-finals of the 1970 World Cup and the 1972 European Championship. He acrimoniously lost the England job, following the team's failure to qualify for the 1974 World Cup.

After managing England, Ramsey briefly held football-related roles at Birmingham City and Panathinaikos, before retiring in 1979–80. Sir Alf Ramsey's statue was dedicated at the reconstructed Wembley Stadium in 2009. He is the first person to be inducted into the English Football Hall of Fame twice – in 2002, in recognition of his achievements as a manager and again in 2010 as a player.

Alf's parents –
Herbert Henry Ramsey and Florence Bixby

Alf's father Herbert Henry Ramsey was born on 31 January 1890 in Dagenham village, Essex to parents John Ramsey and Rosanna Kemp (Romford, 4A/329). In 1891, Herbert H, 1, resided in Becontree Heath, Dagenham, with father John Ramsey, 32, a general dealer, mother Rosanna, 29, and his siblings. In 1901, Herbert, 11, resided in Dagenham, with his widowed father John, 41, a hay and straw dealer, and his siblings. In 1911, Herbert H, 21, a carman, resided in Five Elms, Becontree Heath by Romford, with father John Ramsey, 52, still a widowed hay and straw dealer, sister

Lillian Dorothy, 27, keeping house, and brother Sydney W, 22, also a carman.

Alf's mother Florence Bixby aka Florrie was born on 10 July 1895 in Dagenham to parents Samuel Bixby and Fanny Ainsworth (Romford, 4A/428). In 1901, Florrie, 5, at Clay Cottages, Dagenham, with her father Samuel Bixby, 39, a railway labourer, mother Fanny, 32, and her siblings.

Herbert Henry Ramsey, a manual labourer, married Florence Bixby on Christmas Day, 25 December 1915, during WWI, at St Peter and St Paul Church, Dagenham (Romford, 4A/1567). Herbert and Florrie had six children in Dagenham; Albert W H aka Bert (b. 5 July 1916), Leonard V aka Len (b. 1 May 1918), Alfred Ernest aka Alf (b. 22 January 1920), Winifred M aka Winnie (b. 3 Q. 1923, died 1924), Cyril H (b. 23 February 1925) and Joyce M (b. 2 Q. 1928). Son Alfred Ernest Ramsey was born on 22 January 1920 at 6 Parrish Cottages, Halbutt Street, Dagenham, still an agricultural village in Essex (Romford, 4A/1329). Herbert and Florrie's daughter Winifred, only a few months old, died in 2nd Quarter 1924.

After WWI, Herbert Ramsey was a manual labourer, keeping a smallholding with pigs and driving a horse-drawn dustcart for the council. The family lived at 6 Parrish Cottages, Dagenham, lacking hot water and electricity. The only toilet was outside. Such conditions were typical of Dagenham during this period, although Ramsey's street became an anachronism.

From 1921, London County Council transformed the area into the vast Becontree suburban housing estate. By

1934 it was home to 120,000 residents and the massive Ford Dagenham automobile factory. Parrish Cottages remained untouched. Electricity was not installed until the 1950s, and even then only with Florrie's reluctant approval. She was terrified of the new-fangled technology.

In 1939 War Register, Herbert H Ramsey, born 31 January 1890, a dustman doing heavy work, still at 6 Parrish Cottages, Halbutt Street, Dagenham, with wife Florence, born 10 July 1895, doing unpaid domestic duties, sons Albert W H, born 5 July 1916, a general labourer, Leonard V, born 1 May 1918, a general labourer, Alfred E, born 22 January 1920, a Co-op grocery shop assistant, and Cyril H, born 23 February 1925, a button factory hand.

Herbert Henry Ramsey, 75, died in 1966 (Barking, 5A/27). He died just a few months before his son Alf secured his place in history, leading England to World Cup glory. Florrie lived to see Alf's greatest triumph and Florence Ramsey nee Bixby, 83, died in 1979 (Barking, 11/88).

Alf's paternal grandparents – John Ramsey and Rosanna Kemp

Alf's paternal grandfather John Ramsey (or Ramsay) was born on 7 November 1858 in Levington and baptized in Nacton, Suffolk to parents James Ramsey and Eliza Rattle aka Mary (Woodbridge, 4A/535). In 1861, John, 2, resided on Inn Street, Levington, with father James Ramsey, 36, an agricultural labourer, mother Mary, 33, and his siblings. In 1871, John, 12, an agricultural labourer, resided in a cottage near Hall Farm, Capel St Mary, Ipswich, Suffolk, with father James Ramsey, 43, an agricultural labourer, wife Elizabeth, 38, an agricultural labourer's wife, and his brother William, 14, an agricultural labourer. By 1881, having moved to Dagenham, Essex, John Ramsey, 21, an agricultural labourer, boarded at the family home of James Knight, 30, a hay and straw dealer, of Whalebone Lane, Dagenham. John became a hay and straw dealer on his own account, having learned the trade from James Knight and his father-in-law, Isaac Kemp.

Alf's grandmother Rosanna Kemp (aka Rose Ann or Roshana) was born in December 1861 in Dagenham, Essex to parents Isaac Kemp, a straw dealer, and Eliza Archer. Rosanna was baptized on 29 December 1861 in St Peter and St Paul Church. In 1871, Roshana, 9, a scholar, resided in Becontree Heath, Dagenham, with father Isaac Kemp, 56, a straw dealer, mother Eliza, 54, and her siblings. In 1881, Rosanna, 19, still resided there with her widowed father Isaac Kemp, 67, a straw dealer, and her niece Mary Ann Kemp, 13.

John Ramsey married Rosanna Kemp on 25 September 1883 at Forest Gate, Emmanuel, Essex. They had 5 known children in Dagenham; Lillian Dorothy (b. ~1884), Walter J (b. ~1885), James J (b. ~1887), Sydney W (b. ~1889) and Herbert Henry (b. 2 Q. 1890). Son Herbert Henry Ramsey was born in 2nd Quarter 1890 in Dagenham village to parents John Ramsey and Rosanna Kemp (Romford, 4A/329).

In 1891, John Ramsey, 32, a general dealer, resided in Becontree Heath, Dagenham, with wife Rosanna, 29, children Lillian R, 7, a scholar, Walter J, 6, a scholar, James J and Sydney W, both 2, and Herbert H, 1. Rose Ann Ramsey aka Kemp, 33, died in 1895 in Dagenham (Romford, 4A/252). Rosanna was buried on 3 March 1895 in St Peter and St Paul churchyard, Dagenham. In 1901, John Ramsey, 41, a widowed hay and straw dealer, resided in Dagenham, with his children Lillian, 17, James, 14, Sidney, 12, and Herbert, 11. In 1911, John Ramsey, 52, still a widowed hay and straw dealer, resided in Five Elms, Becontree Heath by Romford, with children Lillian Dorothy, 27, keeping house, Sydney W, 22, a carman, and Herbert H, 21, also a carman.

John Ramsey, 53, died in April 1913 and he buried in St Peter and St Paul churchyard, Dagenham (Romford, 4A/391). During WWI, his son Walter Ramsey enlisted as Private 4609 in the Essex Regiment. Walter later transferred to the Border Regiment and was awarded the Victory and British War Medals.

Alf's maternal grandparents –
Samuel Bixby and Fanny Louisa Ainsworth

Alf's maternal grandfather Samuel Bixby was born in 2nd Quarter 1863 in Dagenham to parents Thomas Bixby and Charlotte Purkis (Romford, 4A/96). In 1871, Samuel, 8, a scholar, at Tyler's Cottage, Dagenham, with father Thomas

Bixby, 50, a ploughman, mother Charlotte, 48, his siblings and his grandfather John Purkis, 85. His grandmother Fanny Louisa Ainsworth was born in 2nd Quarter 1868 in Barking, Essex to parents Francis Robert Ainsworth and Emma March (Romford, 4A/127). In 1871, Fanny, 2, at Grove Place, Barking, with her father Francis Robert Ainsworth, 31, a factory labourer, mother Emma, 27, and her siblings.

Samuel Bixby married Fanny Ainsworth in 4th Quarter 1889 in Dagenham (Romford, 4A/455). Samuel and Fanny had 5 known children in Dagenham; Thomas (b. ~1892), William (b. ~1894), Florence aka Florrie (b. 10 July 1895), Emily (b. ~1898) and Elsie (b. ~1900). Daughter Florence Bixby aka Florrie was born on 10 July 1895 in Dagenham to parents Samuel Bixby and Fanny Ainsworth (Romford, 4A/428). In 1901, Samuel Bixby, 39, a railway labourer, at Clay Cottages, Dagenham, with wife Fanny, 32, children Thomas, 9, William, 7, Florrie, 5, Emily, 3, and Elsie, 1.

In WWI, Samuel and Fanny's son William Bixby enlisted as Private 24684 in the Essex Regiment. William transferred to the Royal Welsh Fusiliers and was awarded the Victory and British War medals. Son Thomas Bixby also served as a Private in the Machine Gun Corps. Fanny Louisa Bixby nee Ainsworth, 75, died in 1943, during WWII, in Dagenham (Romford, 4A/341). Samuel Bixby, 86, died in 1951 (Thurrock, 4A/1147).

Alf's paternal great-grandparents – James Ramsey and Eliza Rattle

Alf's paternal great-grandfather James Ramsey was born around 1827 in Martlesham, Suffolk. His great-grandmother Elizabeth Rattle aka Eliza or Mary was born around 1828 in Nacton, Ipswich, Suffolk. James Ramsey married Eliza Rattle on 8 March 1850 in Grundisburgh, Suffolk. They had 5 known children; Mary (b. ~1851, Nacton), James (b. ~1854, Nacton), William (b. ~1856, Levington), John (b. 7 November 1858, Levington) and Emma E (b. ~1860, Levington). Son John Ramsey was born on 7 November 1858 in Levington and baptized in Nacton, Suffolk to parents James Ramsey and Eliza Rattle.

In 1861, James Ramsey, 36, an agricultural labourer, in Inn Street, Levington, with wife (Eliza or) Mary, 33, children Mary, 10, a scholar, James, 7, a scholar, William, 5, a scholar, John, 2, and Emma E, 1 month old. In 1871, James Ramsey, 43, an agricultural labourer, resided in a cottage near Hall Farm, Capel St Mary, Ipswich, Suffolk, with wife Elizabeth, 38, an agricultural labourer's wife, sons William, 14, and John, 12, both agricultural labourers.

James Ramsey, 60, died 1st Quarter 1886 (Romford, 4A/187) and wife Elizabeth Ramsey nee Rattle, 77, died in 4th Quarter 1905 (West Ham, 4A/142).

Alf's paternal great-grandparents –
Isaac Kemp and Eliza Archer

Alf's paternal great-grandfather Isaac Kemp was born around 1814 and his great-grandmother Eliza Archer was born around 1817 both in Dagenham. Isaac Kemp married Eliza Archer on 25 March 1837 in St Peter and St Paul Church. Isaac and Eliza had 7 known children in Dagenham; Fanny (b. ~1845), Selena, (b. ~1849), Ann (b. ~1851), John (b. ~1854), William (b. ~1856), Rosanna (b. 29 December 1861) and Mary J (b. ~1866).

In 1848, Isaac Kemp, 36, appeared in the Essex Court of Session accused of larceny. However, he was found not guilty and acquitted. In 1861, Isaac Kemp, 46, a straw dealer, resided in Becontree Heath, Dagenham, with wife Eliza, 44, children Selena, 12, Ann, 10, John, 7, and William, 5, all scholars. Daughter Rosanna Kemp (aka Rose Ann or Roshana) was born in December 1861 in Dagenham, Essex to parents Isaac Kemp and Eliza Archer. Rosanna was baptized on 29 December 1861 in St Peter and St Paul Church.

In 1871, Isaac Kemp, 56, a straw dealer, resided in Becontree Heath, Dagenham, with wife Eliza, 54, children Fanny, 26, John, 17, William, 15, both straw dealers' labourers, Roshana, 9, a scholar, and Mary J, 4, a scholar. Eliza Kemp nee Archer, 60, died in October 1877 and was buried on 19 October 1877 in St Peter and St Paul churchyard, Dagenham.

In 1881, Isaac Kemp, 67, a widowed straw dealer, still resided there with his daughter Rosanna, 19, and granddaughter Mary Ann Kemp, 13. Isaac Kemp, 75, a straw dealer, died in March 1890 and was buried on 11 March 1890 in St Peter and St Paul churchyard, Dagenham.

Alf's maternal great-grandparents – Thomas Bixby and Charlotte Purkis

Alf's maternal great-grandfather Thomas Bixby was born on 14 June 1822 in Long Melford, Suffolk. His great-grandmother Charlotte Purkis was born around 1823 in Dagenham, Essex to her father John Purkis. Charlotte's father John Purkis, Alf's maternal great-great-grandfather, was born around 1786 in Sturmer, Essex near Haverhill. Thomas and Charlotte had 3 known sons in Dagenham; Thomas (b. ~1848), William (b. ~1860) and Samuel (b. 2 Q. 1863). In 1871, Thomas Bixby, 50, a ploughman, at Tyler's Cottage, Dagenham, with wife Charlotte, 48, children Thomas, 23, a ploughman, William, 11, an unemployed labourer, Samuel, 8, a scholar, and father-in-law John Purkis, 85. Thomas Bixby, 73, died in 1896 in Samford, Suffolk. His wife Charlotte Bixby nee Purkis, 77, died in 1899 in Whitechapel, London.

Alf's maternal great-grandparents –
Francis Robert Ainsworth and Emma March

Alf's other maternal great-grandfather Francis Robert Ainsworth was born around 1838 in Dagenham, Essex. His great-grandmother Emma March was born around 1842 also in Dagenham. Francis Ainsworth married Emma March in 2nd Quarter 1865 (Romford, 4A/44). Francis and Emma had 3 known children in Barking; William Henry (b. ~1866), Fanny Louisa (b. 2 Q. 1868) and Mary Ann (b. ~1870).

Daughter Fanny Louisa Ainsworth was born in 2nd Quarter 1868 in Barking to parents Francis Robert Ainsworth and Emma March (Romford, 4A/127). In 1871, Francis Robert Ainsworth, 31, a factory labourer, at Grove Place, Barking, with wife Emma, 27, children William Henry, 5, Fanny, 2, and Mary Ann, 1. Emma Ainsworth, 48, died in 1890 in Romford, Essex and husband Francis Robert Ainsworth, 64, died in 1902 in Whitechapel, London.

CONCLUSION

First and foremost, this book is a celebration of the achievement of a group of young Englishmen who, 57 years ago on 30 July 1966, achieved the extraordinary feat of winning the FIFA World Cup, lifting the Jules Rimet Trophy at Wembley. Never again in the annals of English football are we likely to see a team of such humble backgrounds. They were all born in working class towns and villages and marched on to win world football's most prized trophy.

The family histories of the players demonstrate the humility of their ancestral origins. These were men and women who criss-crossed England to scratch a meagre living as agricultural labourers, coal miners, railwaymen, mill workers and domestic servants throughout the Dickensian Victorian era. Poverty-stricken people who emigrated from Ireland to escape famine and destitution in the mid-19th century. Terrified Jews who fled from Eastern Europe in the 19th century to escape Russian Imperialism, Tsarist dominance and religious persecution.

Into the 20th century, the family histories relate struggles to survive during two devastating World Wars and the desperate poverty during the Great Depression of the 1930s. In many ways the family histories of these men and women are no different from our own family histories. Most of us can trace our ancestry back to humble beginnings throughout the Agrarian and Industrial Revolutions. What defines this book is the culmination of these specific family histories in producing a squad of 22 remarkable young men. They went on to 'bring home' what was arguably the greatest English sporting achievement of the 20th century. 'Football's coming home' is the eternal chant of England fans. These were the young men who actually achieved the dream.

In conclusion, this book celebrates the Three Lions.

Player References

Banksy: My Autobiography, Gordon Banks, Les Scott, 2002

George Cohen: My Autobiography, George Cohen, Ben Cohen, James Lawton, 2003

My Life in Soccer, Ray Wilson, 1969

Nobby Stiles: After the Ball – My Autobiography, Nobby Stiles, 2003

Jack Charlton: The Autobiography, Jack Charlton, 1996

Bobby Moore: The Man in Full, Matt Dickinson, 2015

Alan Ball: The Man in White Boots, David Tossell, 2017

My England Years: The Autobiography, Bobby Charlton, 2014

1966 And All That: The Autobiography, Geoff Hurst, 2006

The Ghost of '66: The Autobiography, Martin Peters, 2006

Roger Hunt: Sir Roger, I. John, 2021

Genealogical References

Statutory Registrations of Births, Marriages and Deaths, Census Records and Old Parish Registers: General Register Office, London

1901 and 1911 censuses: National Archives of Ireland, census.nationalarchives.ie

Association of Scottish Genealogists and Researchers in Archives (ASGRA)

Association of Genealogists and Researchers in Archives (AGRA)

Ancestry.co.uk

Familysearch.org

Findmypast.co.uk

Ian Marson, AGRA / ASGRA member (Ref. Gordon Banks probate research)

FreeCEN.co.uk

FreeBMD.co.uk

FreeREG.co.uk

Jewishgen.org

Online and Other References

National Archives, UK, Kew, London

National Records of Scotland, GRH, Edinburgh

Glasgow City Archive, Mitchell Library, Glasgow

Wikipedia.co.uk

Surname Database

The Long, Long, Trail WWI

Hart's Annual Army List

Birminghamhistory.co.uk

ScotlandsPlaces.gov.uk

Runnymede.org.uk

Queenwood Golf Club

The London Times

The London Standard

Amazon.co.uk

British Listed Buildings

Thehuntshouse.com (A-Z Old to New London Street Names)

Sandysrowsynagogue.org

Bishopgate Institute Archives

Glossary of Players' Origin of Surnames

Chapter 1: Banks – this surname, with variant spellings Bankes and Banker, derives from the Northern Middle English "bank(e)", itself coming from the Old Norse "banke" meaning a ridge or hillside, and was originally given as a topographical name to someone who lived on the slope of a hillside or by a riverbank. The final "s" in the name preserves the Olde English genitive ending, i.e., "son of the bank".

Chapter 2: Cohen – this ancient surname has two distinct possible origins, the first being of Gaelic origin, which can be ruled out, as the name is of Ukrainian Jewish origin. The second is Jewish from the Hebrew "kohen", a priest. However, not all Jews bearing this name belong to the priestly caste, descended from Aaron, the brother of Moses. Several members of the faith changed their names to Cohen to avoid forced military service in the Russian Imperial army. Priests were the only males exempt from service.

Chapter 3: Wilson – this distinguished surname, with more than seventy Coats of Arms, is of early mediaeval English origin, recorded throughout the British Isles. It is a patronymic form of the male given name Will, itself a diminutive of William. Introduced into England by William, Duke of Normandy, and known as "The Conqueror", William soon became the most popular given name in England. The Norman form used by the Conqueror, was "Willelm", a spelling adopted from the Frankish Empire of the 8th century. The name is a compound originally consisting of the elements "wil", meaning strength, and "helm", a helmet.

Chapter 4: Stiles – this interesting surname is of Anglo-Saxon origin, and has two possible sources, both topographical. The first is derived from Olde English pre-7th century "stigol" a steep ascent, from "stigan", to climb. The second source is from Olde English "stigel", a stile; in both cases it was given to a person who lived near these places. Topographical surnames were among the earliest created, since both natural and man-made features in the landscape provided easily recognisable names.

Chapter 5 & 8: Charlton – this is an English locational surname from one of numerous places, e.g., Charlton in Berkshire, Hampshire, Sussex, Wiltshire, Northumberland, Somerset etc. In this case, it is almost certainly from Northumberland Charlton. The name derives from Olde English pre-7th century "ceorl" meaning a "peasant" or "serf" and "tun", a "farm" or "settlement". Olde English "ceorlatun" means "settlement of the peasants".

Chapter 6: Moore – this distinguished British surname is recorded in a wide range of spellings including: More, Mores, Moor, Moores, Moors, and in Scotland Muir, and has a number of possible origins. In this case it is a topographical surname for someone who lived on a moor or in a fen, both denoted by Olde English pre-7th century word "mor", or from one of the various villages so named such as Moore in Cheshire, or More in Shropshire.

Chapter 7: Ball – This interesting surname has many possible derivations. Firstly, it may be of early mediaeval English origin, from a nickname for a short, rounded person, taken from Middle English "bal(le)", ball, a development of Olde

English pre-7th century "bealla", and influenced by Old Norse "bollr". In some cases the name may have referred to a bald man, from the same word used in the sense of a round, hairless patch on the skull. Interestingly, the modern English term "bald" derives from a contracted form of Middle English "ballede", from "bal(le)" with "ede", i.e., "having a balle". Secondly, the surname Ball may be topographical in origin, from the same term, "bal(le)", used in the transferred sense of denoting someone who lived on a knoll or rounded hill. Finally, Ball may derive from the Old Norse personal name "Balle", of obscure etymology, but believed to be derived from "bal", torture, pain, or the Olde German personal name "Balle", from "bald", meaning bold.

Chapter 9: Hurst – recorded in the spellings of Hurst, Herst, Hearst, and Hirst, this is an Olde English surname. It is either a topographical name for someone who lived on a wooded hill, derived from Olde English pre-7th century word "hyrst", or as a locational name from one of the various places called Hurst, in Berkshire, Kent, Somerset, and Warwickshire, or Hirst in Northumberland and the West Riding of Yorkshire.

Chapter 10: Peters – recorded as Peter, and patronymics Peters and Peterson, this is an old Crusader surname. It was originally biblical and introduced into Europe by Crusader knights and pilgrims returning from the Holy Land in the 12th century. It derives from the Greek word "petros", meaning a rock, and is associated with St Peter, the apostle. It was first recorded in England as a personal name, as there were no specific surnames, in the Domesday Book of 1086. The final "s" in the name preserves Olde English genitive ending, i.e., "son of Peter".

Chapter 11: Hunt – this ancient surname is pre-7th century English. It is usually an occupational surname for someone who hunts wildlife for a living. In the Middle-Ages the term "hunter" was an official title, and there were different categories from game hunters on foot to mounted huntsmen, who pursued deer and boar. The penalty for hunting without permission in royal parks was death. "Hunta" was sometimes used as a personal name.

Chapter 12: Springett – this interesting, rare and unusual surname is of Anglo-Saxon origin, and is a diminutive nickname for a lively, nimble person. The diminutive suffix "ette", denotes the "son of" or "little" and it was given to a young man. The name derives from Olde English pre-7th century "springan", meaning to jump, or leap, also found in Springer.

Chapter 12: Bonetti – the Italian surname Bonetti was created from the personal name Bona, derived from the Latin name Bonus, meaning "good", with "etti" being the diminutive of the name denoting "son of" or "little". The popularity of the personal name Bonus, was in part due to the name held by a 3rd century Christian saint, martyred in Rome. The surname Bonetti was first recorded in Milan around 1220.

Chapter 12: Armfield – recorded in a number of spellings including Armfield, Armfeeld, Armfeild and Armefeild, this surname is English. It is of locational origin from a place spelt "Earmfeld" or similar, and appears to be one of the many "lost" mediaeval villages in Britain. The original site is believed to have been in Yorkshire. The name appears

66

to have the unusual meaning of "land of the outlaws", from Olde English words "earm" meaning wretched, but used in the sense of outlaws, and "feld" in the original sense describing open country.

Chapter 12: Byrne – recorded as O'Byrne but more commonly as Byrne, this is an Irish surname of high antiquity. Claiming descent from Bran, the king of Leinster, who died in 1052, this great clan originated in County Kildare. They held extensive territory until the Anglo-Norman invasion of Ireland in 1169-1170, when they migrated to County Wicklow, occupying the country between Rathdrum and Shillelagh. The name in Irish Gaelic is O'Broin, meaning the male descendant of Bran, meaning the raven.

Chapter 12: Hunter – recorded as Huntar, Hunter, and the female Huntress and Huntriss, this ancient surname is of Anglo-Scottish origin. The derivation is from Olde English pre-7th century word "hunta", from "huntian", meaning to hunt, with the suffix "er", meaning one who hunts or works with a hunter. The term was used not only by hunters on horseback of game such as stags and wild boars, a pursuit in the Middle Ages restricted to the nobility, but also as a nickname for bird catchers and poachers.

Chapter 12: Callaghan – this ancient and honourable Irish name is an Anglicized form of the Gaelic "O'Ceallachain" composed of the elements "Og" meaning "descendant of" plus "Ceallachain", a diminutive of the personal name "Ceallach" meaning contention or strife. This name was held by a 10th century King of Munster, from whom many present day surname bearers claim descent.

Chapter 12: Flowers – this surname has two distinct possible sources. In the first instance, Flowers may have originated as a patronymic form of the mediaeval nickname "Flo(u)r" from the Middle English "flor" via the Old French "flur", a flower. This was a conventional term of endearment in mediaeval romantic poetry. As early as the 13th century it was also used as a female given name. The surname may also derive from an occupational name for an arrow maker. This derivation is from the Middle English "flo", a development of Olde English pre-7th century "fla", an arrow, with the addition of the ancient "er" – an arrow maker.

Chapter 12: Connelly – this interesting Irish surname, with variant spellings O' Connolly, Conneely, O'Conley, etc., is an Anglicized form of the old Gaelic prefix "Og" meaning "son of", and the personal name Conghaile, from "con", a hound, and "gal", valour, hence, "son of the hound of valour". The O' Conghailes were an ancient Connacht sept who dispersed into three main branches in Meath, Monaghan and Munster.

Chapter 12: Eastham – recorded as Easton, Eastam, and Eastham, this surname is early English. It is locational from any of the numerous places thus called, e.g., Isle of Wight, Devon, Essex and Northamptonshire. The name originates from Olde English pre-7th century elements, "east" meaning to the east plus the suffix "tun" or "ham". However, there are other meanings, and for instance Easton in Essex derives its name from Olde English "ege" meaning "island", plus "stan(as)", stones. Eastham originates from

Eastham, a village near Chester, in Cheshire, or Eastham in Worcestershire.

Chapter 12: Greaves – this interesting surname is of Anglo-Saxon origin, and has two possible sources. Firstly, the surname may be locational, i.e., a Lancashire place name. It derives from Olde English pre-7th century "graefe", grove or thicket. Locational surnames were developed when former inhabitants of a place moved to another area and were identified by their birthplace. Secondly, the surname may have been topographical for a "dweller by the grove", from the same derivation as before. Topographical surnames were among the earliest created, since features in the landscape provided easily recognisable names.

Chapter 12: Paine – this name derives from the personal name "Pagen", popularly known as Paine or Payne. It comes from the Old French "paien" or Latin "paganus" originally meaning "a villager or rustic", and later corrupted to mean a heathen or non-Christian. As a personal name it was first recorded in the Domesday Book of 1086.

Chapter 13: Ramsey – this distinguished surname, having no less than ten Coats of Arms, is of Anglo-Saxon origin, and is a locational name either from Ramsey, a market-town and parish in Huntingdonshire, or from the parish and village of Ramsey, south west of Harwich in Essex, the latter being the more likely in this case. The former place, recorded as "Hramesege" in the Saxon Chartulary, dated circa 1000, is so called from Olde English pre-7th century "hramsa", wild garlic, ramson, with "ege", island, piece of firm land in a fen, or land situated between streams; hence, "wild garlic island".

The latter place, appearing as "Rameseia" in the Domesday Book of 1086, and as "Rammesye" in the 1224 Feet of Fines for Essex, shares the same meaning and derivation.

ABOUT THE AUTHOR

Derek Niven is a pseudonym used by John McGee, an ASGRA member, for factual and genealogical publications. Derek Beaugarde is known for his science fiction publications. John McGee was born in 1956 in Corkerhill railway village, Glasgow, attending Mosspark Primary and Allan Glen's schools. The late actor Sir Derek Bogarde spent three unhappy years at Allan Glen's as a pupil named Derek Niven van den Bogaerde. Therefore, the observant reader will readily discern the origin of the two pseudonyms.

After spending 34 years in the rail industry in train planning and accountancy John McGee retired in 2007. In 2012 the idea for his science fiction novel emerged. 2084: The End of Days © Derek Beaugarde was published by Corkerhill Press in 2016. In the years leading up to 2084, seven disparate men and women across the globe battle with their own personal frailties and human tragedies. Suddenly, they are drawn together to fight for survival against the ultimate global disaster – Armageddon!

2084: The End of Days is available on Amazon websites.

Other books in the Pride Series
by Derek Niven:-

Pride of the Lions: the untold story of the men and women who made the Lisbon Lions, Derek Niven © 2017

Pride of the Jocks: the untold story of the men and women who made the greatest Scottish managers © Derek Niven, 2018

Pride of the Bears: the untold story of the men and women who made the Barça Bears © Derek Niven, 2020

Pride of the Hearts: the untold story of the men and women who made the Great War heroes of Heart of Midlothian © Derek Niven, 2021

PRIDE OF THE LIONS

The untold story of the men and women
who made the Lisbon Lions

DEREK NIVEN

PRIDE OF THE JOCKS

The untold story of the men and women
who made the greatest Scottish football managers

DEREK NIVEN
Foreword by Kathleen Murdoch

PRIDE OF THE BEARS

The untold story of the men and women
who made the Barça Bears

DEREK NIVEN

PRIDE OF THE HEARTS

The untold story of the men and women who made
the Great War heroes of Heart of Midlothian

DEREK NIVEN

Milton Keynes UK
Ingram Content Group UK Ltd.
UKHW040321111123
432358UK00004B/100